Victory for the Soul

Relationships that Work

Gordon Corwin II
and Saint Germain

Highland Light Publishers Edition 2022

Oceanside, CA. 92056-6237

COPYRIGHT Gordon Corwin II Lah Rahn Ananda

ALL RIGHTS RESERVED
INCLUDING THE RIGHT OF REPRODUCTION
IN WHOLE OR IN PART IN ANY FORM

HIGHLAND LIGHT PUBLISHERS IS
A REGISTERED TRADEMARK WITH THE U. S. PATENT
AND TRADEMARK OFFICE. GORDON W. CORWIN II

2022 First Edition Highland Light
Publishers

All rights reserved. No part of this book may be used or reproduced by any means, graphic, electronic, or mechanical Including photocopying, recording, taping, or by any information storage retrieval system.

This Book "Victory for the Soul, *Relationships that Work*" may be ordered through Amazon.com or **by visiting the Author's website:**

www.SaintGermainChronicles.com
or through independent and chain book sellers, online retailers worldwide.

The views expressed in this book are conditioned by the Disclaimer which follows. Certain stock imagery © Dreamstime.com., 123RF.com and Gordon W. Corwin II.

ISBN 978-0-9914924-2-8

Saint Germain

Portrait Marius Fine Art

Books by This Author

৽৶ ৵৽

THE SAINT GERMAIN CHRONICLES COLLECTION
A Journey Into Practical Spirituality

VICTORY FOR THE SOUL
Relationships That Work

RISING ABOVE
A Journey To Higher Dimensions

ANGER HEALING AND TRANSMUTATION
An Elevation Of The Soul

TRUE GRATITUDE - Quan Yin

Contents

Overview 1
Chapter 1:   Approaching Relationship 11
Chapter 2:   Inside Your Personal Universe 25
Chapter 3:   Partnership Dynamics 31
Chapter 4:   Self-Love 39
Chapter 5:   Patience 69
Chapter 6:   Sëlf-Talk 83
Chapter 7:   Discovering Your Triggers 101
Chapter 8:   Emotions 119
Chapter 9:   Change 143
Chapter 10: Forgiveness and Compassion 155
Chapter 11: Communication 161
Chapter 12: Creating Space for Us and We 171
Chapter 13: Perspectives About Us 191
Chapter 14: Adulthood 217
Chapter 15: Attachment 221
Chapter 16: A Personal Experience 237
Chapter 17: Detachment 241
Chapter 18: Moving On 269
Chapter 19: Gratitude 277
Chapter 20: Changing Competition into Oneness 279
Chapter 21: *SaintGermain's* Inspiration to the Author 303
Chapter 22: *SaintGermain* Quotations from this Book 309
Disclaimer: 333
Light of the Soul Foundation 501(c)(3) 335
Acknowledgements 339
About the Author 343
Index 347

OVERVIEW

"Energy and persistence conquer all things"

Benjamin Franklin

The heartbeat of true Relationship between You, Me and We is located at the core of Oneness, where *'Victory For The Soul'* comes into Being. This union is the glue that creates a magically blended space of flourishing Relationship Unity.

    The gift of Soul to Soul of relationships can bring the finest opportunities to find Love, happiness, and fulfillment, as you grow and rise to the pinnacle of Mastering the Life's Lessons handed to you, often through involvement with others. Along this path of Practical Spirituality, certain *Liberations from the Human Condition* are your well-deserved rewards of Mastery, My Dear Friends.

As Spirit shines Light and words of Wisdom upon the *dynamic interplay* between pulsating consciousnesses of relationship partners and the dance that follows, you will surely be enlightened! Revealed here are the many faces of Relationship. Through this gateway of Wisdom you can know and own these ultimate gifts of evolvement and personal growth ... as yours.

This Book *'Victory For The Soul, Relationships that Work'*, encompasses the awareness, art, skill, and the discipline of mixing together aligned fun, pleasures, visions, Love and compassion, emotions, anger, forgiveness, communication, change, gratitude, shared aspirations, responsibilities, mutual interests, and yes, some bumpy challenges along the way, ... plus a vast multitude of compelling relationship topics still remaining at the forefront of Humanity's attention over the ages.

It is the intention of Spirit and of the Author as Spirits' appointed instrument and vessel, that this work guide you through applying fundamental and positive partnership dynamics. This includes integrating essential pieces of the relationship puzzle that deeply influence and touch vital parts of an evolving lifetime open to self-examination and change. We Ascended pray this is you!

Openness to Mastering higher vibrational possibilities is emphasized in many various aspects of Relationship. Surely you have noticed issues that *repeatedly* show up in your life-stream, often having the same pattern, yet no solution(s) in sight? Recognizing your choices and behaviors of resistance to *change* ...

along with opening needed space for Mastery of the relationship issue(s) at hand ... is the healing focus of this book.

Throughout, We in Spirit and the Author, as Our Instrument and now one of the Saint Germain Earth Partners, ... are together here addressing many interlocking parts of a mind-numbing puzzle presented to you in these 22 Chapters. We intend that this Wisdom flow to you sequentially, understandable by Earthly consciousness. Thus, We lovingly guide you through these full spectrum highlights presented in *'Victory for the Soul, Relationships that Work'*.

Here are core fundamentals of Relationship that can lead you beyond raw Ego and out of common status quo breakdown spirals into new territories of harmony, togetherness, mutual contribution and Love. *With an open hand, you can Be a giver with ease and grace to create this space to receive Gifts for the Soul from one or more partners that hold a meaningful vibration and share basic values.* Here We address the 'We' of a 'You' and 'Me' mind-set!

That said, core fundamentals are energized into Chapters, titled and organized to stimulate *your*

The Universe, Spirit and Karma will soon enough show you the alignment of *your truth* with Universal Truth!

Let them be in synch!

---

individual inquiry into your own consciousness and belief

system, ... with latitude *to authentically fill in the blanks as 'your truth' for now ... as revealed from you to you! Here is the place you begin mining the gold and uncovering what is next for you in your Grand Process of Truth.*

We address here relationships of all sorts, recognizing that partnerships have many faces and varieties, which can embrace Spirit, marriage, Lovers, friends, families, business, etc.

At first blush, wide-eyed and sometimes blinding enthusiasm of a new relationship can be overpowering. Snap decisions to become deeply involved are tempting, especially when physical and romantic attractions are throbbing high on the list. Here, *a useful pause* can save you much heartache down the road. Meanwhile, at this time in your life, you can **choose to begin applying** the **'You Me & We'** **core relationship fundamentals.** We place emphasis also upon openness to *daily healings, so very important to set in place in real time, both at the outset and throughout your relationship journeys.*

When *your emotional triggers are activated by life's lessons, ... handed to you via relationship gifts ...* **this book will show you the way to access building blocks needed to stand upon as you ride the upward spiral into Mastery. We invite you to know building blocks such as Self-Love, Knowing yourself, and Transforming** *certain* **parts of 'Me' into 'Us' and 'We'. You then have axiomatic starters for relationships that can flourish with grand mutual abundance.**

Then come Chapters about integrating Spirit as your third Partner, Accepting Change, Knowing about Needs vs. Wants, and Discovering your Hot Buttons / Emotional Triggers and more ... all to move your expanding consciousness a bit further along the path. Chapters titled Communication, Self-talk, and Forgiveness, come into play as you practice applying the healing solutions to the life's lessons that come your way, *often disguised as everyday events, sometimes mislabeled as co-incidental.* Techniques to arrive at empowering and balanced Win-Win solutions are emphasized throughout the Book.

Patience and it's rewards, along with clear communication, is treated in great detail and tender care, adding new perspectives, a priceless resource for your *tool box in the awareness, art, skill, and discipline of relationship*.

Newly released techniques are unveiled about 'avoiding judgements' and 'avoiding anger' ... while 'embracing forgiveness', as achievable milestones of enlightenment, to personally and fully integrate into consciousness and to use in daily life, now and forever!

You may be aware that Soul Mates are *drawn to each other in the now*, often from relationships in former lifetimes. Here is a chance to balance Karma and align now what two (or more) of you could *not* do in former times, with all the irony and challenge of the present living Human Condition. We encourage you to stay the course, smooth out the wrinkles, and get it Mastered this time around, *while the iron is hot!* And, along the way, ... learn to enjoy those tickling humorous moments that can burst through with welcome laughter relief to brighten these days and nights of your life!

The Journey

Interlocking Spheres of Life Lessons

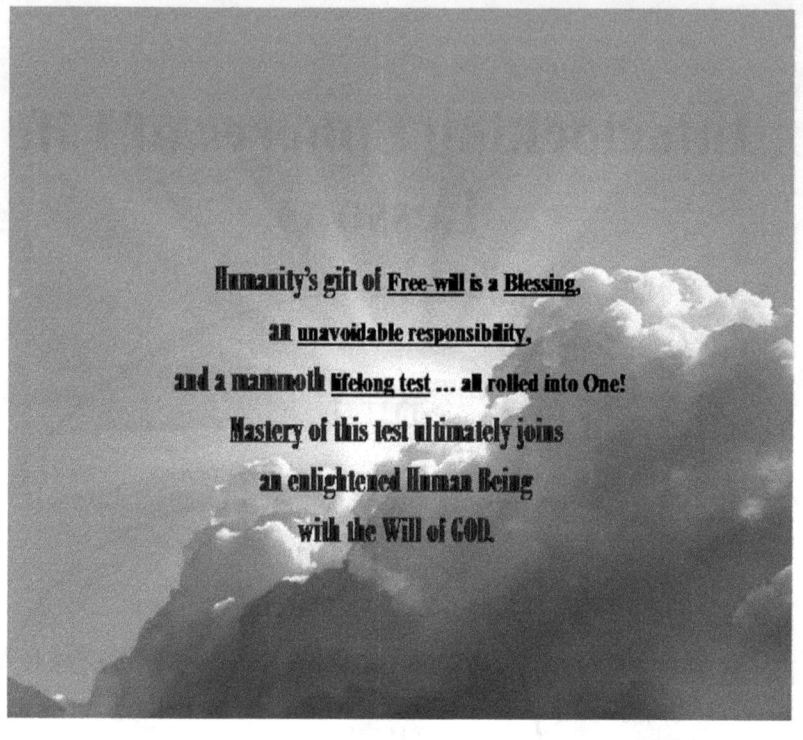

Humanity's gift of Free-will is a Blessing,
an unavoidable responsibility,
and a mammoth lifelong test ... all rolled into One!
Mastery of this test ultimately joins
an enlightened Human Being
with the Will of GOD.

As you journey through this Book, truthfully **writing your own secrets** into the blank spaces provided, We intend that healing insights will frequently appear to you with new introspection and self-honesty. **You will learn** *to turn breakdowns into breakthroughs w*hen milestones are met and Mastered along your path. **As you apply My Wisdom, notice the wondrous Freedom that begins to flow.** *I pray you will experience these euphoric moments of joyful elation and balance, where you are fully enraptured, and yet refrain, …with awareness anchored in place, … from drowning in what is meant to be your ecstasy!*
Mastery of your relationship milestones can then afford you the well-deserved rewards of ever increasing times

of quality life ... in harmony, relaxation and enjoyment of bliss that can be yours!

Many Blessings in the Light,
Saint Germain

And Lah Rahn Ananda
aka Gordon Corwin II

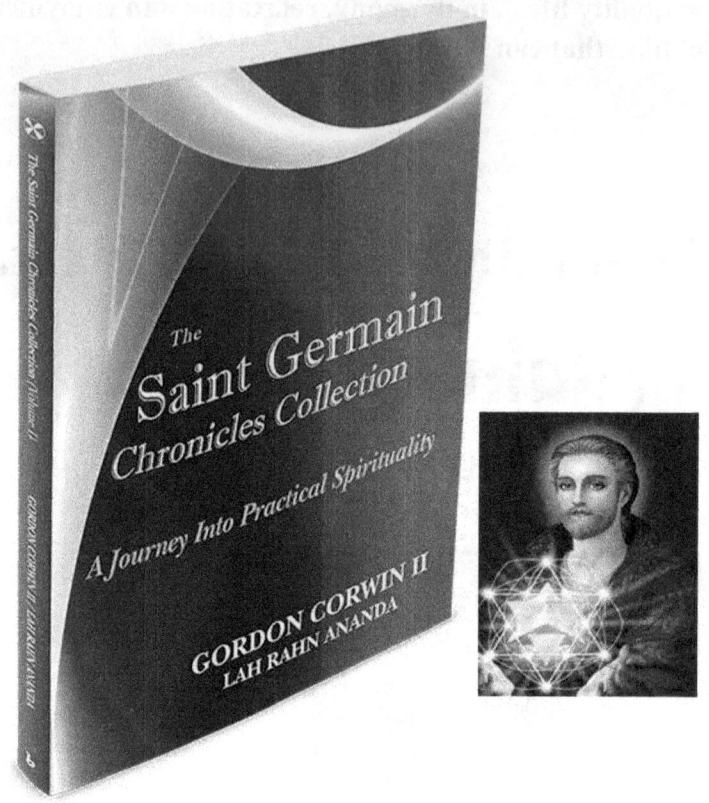

By Master Saint Germain and Gordon Corwin II
released in 2017, Amazon.com

Chapter 1

Approaching Relationship

Visions and Realities

The **fires of passion,** the vigor of new visions, the excitement of new friendships, the flame of romance, the motivation for success on many levels, whatever your incentive, ... commonly drive

Humans to enthusiastically a*pproach relationship.*
Sometimes actions are wise with prior consideration, and sometimes blind, ... when diving in head first!

The intent of this Chapter is to support your engagement in *a genuine optimistic view* of the landscape you are approaching, yet with awareness of need to control emotions that may otherwise find you on a slippery slope! We discuss below some of *the many profound elements and considerations about beginning a new relationship of any sort, be it business, acquaintance, personal friend, romantic, etc.*

About Desire. **Truly Being in *full-hearted relationship is for those Ones with an innate desire to do so, and the faint of heart need look elsewhere***.

Completely <u>owning</u>, as yours, this reality of engaged dedication is so very important to consciously accept ...<u>to empower your relationship to flourish in well-being</u>. Let this be a guiding truth as you approach.

Approaching Relationship in good faith and trust *is truly a grand commitment, My Dear Ones. It involves some bravery for you to be willing to evolve beyond your Ego's resistance into a full, loving relationship partner. <u>One who is willing</u> to adjust, adapt, and modify prior learned behavior patterns of thought and action, is to be commended indeed, ... as you would openly travel into these new uncharted waters of change. To willingly acquire, with personal ownership, the mindset unveiled throughout this entire book, ... as your guiding Light in relationship, ... opens the gateway for you to approach with a kind and loving heart, gracefully and joyfully surrendering unto your new Self with an open hand.*

Once you have elevated yourself upward onto this wonderful surrendered plateau, living and Being the demonstration partner who blends into consciousness the behaviors and freedoms I describe *will place you, ... mind, body and Soul, in a brilliant new state of vibration. With inspiration and diligence, you will come to appreciate this, perhaps sooner than later!*

As Saint Germain, I predict from Above that your Masterful milestone *victories can well lead* you toward *personal relationship nirvana, a place of joy and freedom for this lifetime and beyond. Such a beautiful gift is your birthright, if only you will choose to receive it, in full ownership of its grandness, My Dearest Friends.*

ॐ

T he **Law of Attraction** has been spoken by enlightened Ones on your plane:

> 'Being a friend of change will strengthen you in facing the inevitable'

> 'When you believe it, you will see it'

> 'When You don't attract what you want, you attract what you are'

Attractions between Humans on a personal level also point to the **Law of Karma. 'Could this be part of my relationship journey' … you ask?** Most definitely. Opportunities to rub next to others are commonly presented by Spirit. Sometimes 'signs' are given to underscore the Karmic energy sent to you. The <u>invitation</u> for you is an opening for growth, with hope that you will <u>recognize and act</u> upon the opportunity at hand. Karma is sometimes part of a life lesson, your bonus!

Family members, business associates, spouses, lovers, friends, and acquaintances are favorites for Spirit to place at your door *as vehicles for Karma to have its way with you and help you Master previously un-Mastered life's lessons in this and in prior lifetimes as well.*

The Law of Karma states *that every action generates a force of energy that returns in like kind.*

Choosing actions that generate love and happiness and Soul growth to others opens the portal for the same energy flowing back to you in kind!

Divine Reciprocity.

If you are *alert and aware,* you will find a way to recognize and engage *with Karmic situations in balancing your Karma through relationship.*

***Realize that* certain meetings** can seem to be 'co-incidental' and appear at first glance to have little significance at that time. Others can be so *and then sometimes develop into profound, <u>unanticipated Karmic reunion </u>(s) of great importance to the life's lessons that you are yet to learn ... and with the company and aid of that certain One that you 'accidentally' met!*

Can you imagine that! We in Spirit work in Our magic ways to bring Karmic balance and Ascension opportunities to Humankind on a regular basis, Folks!

Wise Spirit seekers, as We notice from Above, are aware of Karma in action in the moment. When you reach this level, you too will deeply appreciate this Oneness of All in the Universe!

L et Us consider a few *perspectives of approaching a new relationship.* We pray these viewpoints, and more, will hold you in good stead on firm ground, at least at the outset.

In the beginning, its good to know that *Illusion* often raises its head and has its way with you. Yes, certainly One is understandably optimistic in the inception! This is a healthy, attractive, positive start and one of the very reasons for forming a partnership to begin with. Yes or yes?

We shall call this the first phase, that of relationship <u>*inspiration*</u>**.**

And, of course, ... a wise prospective relationship partner in this looking phase, need be aware that enthusiasm flowing freely, as it often does, *can form into* *illusion, sweeping One off of one's feet,* with expectations over-shining the realities of truth!

These needed realities can be, e.g., the overlooking of some fundamental characteristics or behaviors native to the prospective partner(s), including yourself!

1. Oversights of inconvenient or even ugly truths can be costly in many ways.

And then again, some realities *can turn out to be surprise positives,* empowering and complementary all around you.

How often We Above see mistakes of awareness and perception at the inception!

Notice that illusion raises its head in the 3rd Dimensional realm on Earth, where circumstances are discovered to be at odds with the Truth. Illusion is the grand disguise that covers up!

Quite often in the beginning, in the oooh aaaah stages of the relationship, *illusion clouds the real you, as well as the real partner that has appeared in your life!* Then as time goes on, illusion disappears in favor of reality, and ooooops here come the life's lessons! *And in this case,* perhaps here comes the next phase of this relationship when faces are bared, without masks of illusion.

A word to the wise, Folks. Think, observe, meditate, talk to Us in Spirit … before you leap into the breach!

Consider opening your heart in stages, rather than 'all in' at the first blush of excitement. See what feels aligned to you, as your relationship develops, and as you feel out the effects of certain *relationship structures taking hold, or maybe not? Early agreement to support each other, for example, is a marvelous beginning structure to put in place.*

About the attraction? Your honest <u>assessment</u> *of the 'attraction' is a poignant starting point.*

*What did <u>**your heart tell you**</u> about something special, … at the first blush, the first meeting, the first encounter?*

Be honest with yourself as you write.

_____
_____
_____
_____
_____
_____
_____
_____
_____
_____
_____
_____
_____
_____

What was your first impression? *First impressions are noteworthy, especially if your <u>intuition</u> is developed.*

Was it 'in gear' at that moment?

_____
_____
_____
_____

The motivation? What <u>wants or needs</u> do you feel pushed you on to somehow pursue or *follow through*?

_____
_____
_____
_____
_____
_____
_____
_____
_____
_____
_____

Did you take the time and effort to <u>look in depth</u> to see who this person might really be? What did you find out, (or did you skip this step?)

_____
_____
_____
_____

_____
_____
_____

When consulting _your heart_ ... what are/were your feelings?
_____
_____
_____
_____
_____

In retrospect, what _ILLUSIONS did_ you accept as _realities_ about this person?
_____
_____
_____
_____
_____
_____
_____
_____
_____

Ask 'what did Spirit say' as _guidance about this person_?
Can you Access Spirit? Consult Our instruments for

assistance if you like. They are called Spiritual Channels, Ones such as your current Author.

When using your 3rd Dimensional resources, (internet, library, background history, associates, etc.) what reliable information did you learn? Experiences of others (family, friends …) may also influence you to some extent. *Remember, as you search, Opinions are only Opinions!*

_____
_____
_____
_____
_____
_____
_____
_____
_____

What if this person does not share my religion? In Spirit, We clearly distinguish between 'Truth" and *organizations of various names that would modify Truth with secular beliefs and codes, sometimes called religions.* **Just remember, Truth is Truth! Focus upon and seek the Truth!**

As you proceed in this reality phase, We advise you to go slowly, in as much ease and grace and restraint of over-enthusiasm that you can muster up. Remember patience? Relationships unfold in their own good time, and if you partner with Spirit, the presence and effects of *Divine timing* will become very well known to you!

About Structure. *Somewhere in the beginning,* a heart- to- heart, even exchange of your best positive energies with each other will need to take place. This is also an ideal time to compare your basic values. Then, perhaps it's time for approaching some structure?

Some friendly agreement(s), for example, about how you will interact with each other, a *few* of your <u>wants and needs and of their wants and needs</u>. There may be a temptation to unload too much at once here, so be careful not to crowd the space or smother a partner, here or at any time.

These exchanges can be light-hearted and yet be sincere <u>agreements that need be said to get off on the right foot</u>. Supporting each other, being open about your feelings, showing care and consideration for each other, and *keeping your promises* <u>stand out as agreements that attract responsible aware Ones of integrity and character.</u>

Seeing Resistance here? Well ... maybe take a second look at whom you are dealing with right out of the gate. Better now than later! If you meet resistance on the basics, the red flags should fly high in your consciousness at this point!

Feeling their Vibrations? *Try to get a <u>feeling of this person's energy field</u> and how they vibrate and how compatible this may be with you?*

Your observations?

_____
_____
_____
_____
_____

_____
_____
_____

As your interactions proceed in due time, writing a Relationship Journal (separate from this book) is highly recommended for you to monitor progress as things develop. <u>**Log in and date your entries**</u> such as:

    The joys, happy times, and ecstasy moments,

    The major challenges as they come along,

    Your reactions,

    Your replies, after consideration,

    Patterns of behavior that surface, you and they,

    If there is an upset, name it and note the source.

      What Win-Win solutions came into being?

Your Life's lessons can be healings from each major event that you experience.

As you re-read this book and your journal

note your   progress when you
re-read your   writings in the
blanks   you have filled in.

Alright! We shall now proceed to embrace you with the next Chapter, 'Self-Love'.

Many Blessings along Your Journey.

Saint Germain

And Lah Rahn Ananda aka Gordon Corwin II

Chapter 2

INSIDE YOUR PERSONAL UNIVERSE

Have you dared to take more than a peek inside yourself to see what makes you tick?

If **you only take a brief moment, a time-out from the daily hustle and bustle**, to observe what lies beyond the knee jerk ego reactions that stimulate and control so much of a Human life, you might just be surprised about what lies inside. Do you know what runs you?

Take relationships for starters. *A conscious self-examined life might just reveal some openings about your heart level connections with others, and even Soul connections, ... which could easily be* *separated from motivated Ego connections that carry an agenda, admit it or not. And then, there is sometimes a strange mixture of the two, with possible Soul connection thrown in, to really challenge you! Welcome to the Human Condition, Folks!*

This is where living an examined life can get more complicated and tricky. We remind you that relationships are only one of many facets of a self-examined life, and yet <u>immensely impactive as a primary tool for delivering life's lessons for your evolution!</u>

P**ersonal Relationships**. '*Oh Dear, why does this seem to take front stage center so often in the course of my life?*' 'Should I let this attraction play out, … to start and continue, as transient energies *and* Egos have their way?' 'Is there a structure that I can blend with my emotions to guide me through?'

Of course. And then, in **time, patterns** inevitably **emerge and change**, often resulting in friendships, loves and associations *running through your consciousness as nurturing, or often needing course corrections. Sometimes events run amok, showing you insights how relationship chaos can cunningly creep into the mix, if you allow it.* <u>And, I pray, inspiring you to consciously recognize each life lesson as it is playing out!</u>

Listen and Talk to your Chakras

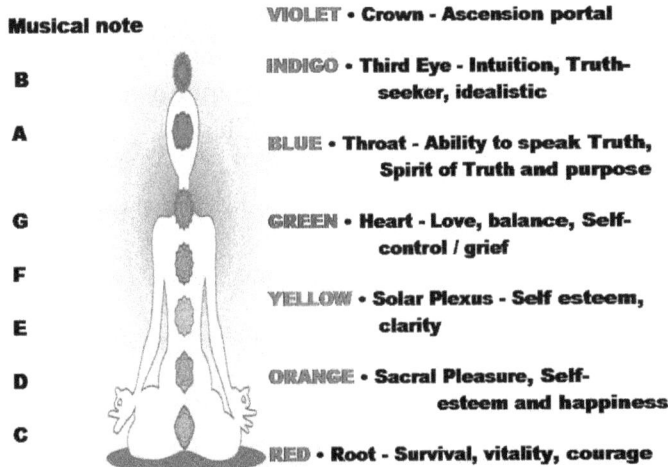

Musical note

- VIOLET • Crown - Ascension portal
- B
- INDIGO • Third Eye - Intuition, Truth-seeker, idealistic
- A
- BLUE • Throat - Ability to speak Truth, Spirit of Truth and purpose
- G
- GREEN • Heart - Love, balance, Self-control / grief
- F
- YELLOW • Solar Plexus - Self esteem, clarity
- E
- D
- ORANGE • Sacral Pleasure, Self-esteem and happiness
- C
- RED • Root - Survival, vitality, courage

    The chakras, or main energy centers of your body, are **interconnecting spiral-chakras that hold physical, mental, emotional and Spiritual energy for you.** These centers of energy react to life experiences as they affect you, voluntarily or involuntarily. So when you consciously make life's choices in alignment with Divine and Universal Law, your chakras react to *this conscious* input from a trained and purified mind, **mirroring how you have chosen to act or react to life as it unfolds.**

    Now, you are able to govern the frequency of your vibration. How did Master Sananda Kumara process and transmit input to his body chakras **to demonstrate Love** as he did? It was through **his conscious choice!** On the contrary, however, a choice to be fearful, angry or violent, ... activates these corresponding lower body chakras. Remember though, **you can catch yourself** and re-choose in an instant when you are sufficiently trained, and your alternate choice in the same situation could then usher you into the upper body chakra vibrations.

    There is the Magic. Now you are a candidate to reach for and **hold the Divine White Light** that allows you *to transcend the duality of your secular world.* Only a cleansed and purified EGO need apply for admission here. So to assist you, that is why We in the Ascended Realm, recommend and insist upon **your daily practice of Decreeing** to re-balance, re-seed, and implant into your consciousness the highest parts of the Positive Vibration Range.

© Copyright 2014 Gordon W. Corwin II. All rights reserved. Contact: Lah@SaintGermainChronicles.org

Notice and note very carefully exactly what attracts you, and vice-versa ... the first encounter. In this *beginning stage, a dance of a yet unknown relationship,* feelings begin to flow, your chakras do their energy movement 'thing', as you would say. Your chakras may be activated and flutter about in response to feelings that flood in. Awareness of your chakras (see below) and the balancing that you can do to yourself, will surely smooth out the process of adapting to inevitable change. Look forward to reading the upcoming Chapter 'Emotions' later in this Book, and My transmission of Chakra Dynamics, soon to be released in RISING ABOVE, A Journey To Higher Dimensions, My next book, Gordon Corwin II 2022 Amazon

As you become increasingly aware of your chakra energies, and their intensities, balancing is clearly your next step. Various techniques, including those of your Earthly Tao, are available to Humanity and I shall leave that erotic conversation to another day ... for those of you *who dare to willingly engage in change sufficiently enough to seek and find your Human Light in the Darkness.*

To willingly work with change, My Dearest Ones, is one of the main catalysts for manifesting into reality the wisdom I offer in MY books and channeled appearances with audiences and to individuals.

I have confidence in your strength and perseverance to forge ahead and let the Light shine brightly upon you ... as you seek, find, and walk your Dharma.

Saint Germain

Through Lah Rahn Ananda aka Gordon Corwin II

'To keep the body in good health is a duty, otherwise we shall not be able to keep our mind strong and clear'.

Buddha

Chapter 3

Partnership Dynamics

Traits of a Successful Partnership

~ Glue and Drama ~

We Ascended are delighted that some of you are already finding these *Traits of a Successful Partnership* to have significant meaning in your lives, progressing forward in grace. The choice to let these Partnership aspects of our Wisdom find a home in your consciousness will surely pay off!

As I begin, please note that these freshly written *Building Blocks'*, are also ripe topics to also be spoken of in some depth and presented in our upcoming live Saint Germain channeled events on **Partnership Dynamics** held in San Diego, Orange County and Los Angeles, and spoken in person through My Spiritual instrument, Lah Rahn Ananda. Also, if you desire a *jump start on building Business Partnerships*, I would direct you to My newly published book, <u>The Saint Germain Chronicles Collection</u>, Gordon Corwin II aka Lah Rahn Ananda,

Amazon Books, 2017 especially the Ninth Chapter, *"Growing to Fill Your Divine Business Shoes"!*

Partnerships have many faces and varieties, which can embrace friends, families, marriages, lovers, Spirit, business, and whichever else you may choose. As you successfully climb up the Spiritual ladder, rung by rung, the priority and importance of your *Spiritual Partnership* will, I guarantee, rise to first place!

Regardless of a Partnership label, business, personal, or otherwise, it is good to know there are certain *recurring common threads that serve as essential elements to glue your relationships together ... and to sustain them in your embrace.*

Often the fire and enthusiasm of the moment can lure you into the flame, Dear Friends, blindly attracting One into forming *or* sustaining a partnership. *Armed with Wisdom herein, success may well be at your doorstep. By now in reading this book, you may recognize that opportunity laced with Wisdom may be knocking also! A relationship in the making, though optimism may be firmly in hand, is wisely viewed for realistic and <u>viable upside potential</u>, as well as for potential illusion, <u>the grey areas</u> that may lurk, for the unaware!*

Fluctuating emotions of your consciousness, eager to have immediate satisfaction, can easily inject enticing stimuli ... *eager to hastily jump into the breach.* These can usually be found seated in Ego, separate from One's Higher-self. The Ego cleverly weighs the options, <u>*tempted* to be detached from the wiser consciousness of Higher-Self and from Spirit's available guidance.</u> (You are not alone in this part of your Process, Dear Ones, <u>your dilemmas and requests thru prayers are heard daily!</u>)

So, in short, even lured by a healthy enthusiasm, a wise *man or woman, young or old,* will heed my Wisdom before acting, **and** during a partnership duration as well!
As dramas may arise, one or more of the Six elements I cite below can be in *ongoing* need of shoring up along the way. You may have experienced this reality? Read on, Dear Ones.

☙❧

The Present Moment

Allowing new moments to unfold without old grudges blocking the way.

  Knowing how to *consciously meld fresh, new present moment openings with your past experiences is so very important to developing your capability to expand without limitation.* I speak here of allowing past experiences, … in this case applied to relationship, … to Be, gracefully lain upon your consciousness in <u>truth</u> (without opinion) … as you create <u>space to receive new moments with an open hand.</u>

  Be forcefully aware that you Humans are so often *tempted to color fresh moments with past experiences by ruthlessly and unconsciously <u>judging and convicting the fresh</u>*

<u>new present moment ... before even knowing what it is or experiencing its potential gift!</u>

Being open-minded *is a learned discipline that is well worth your while, Dear Ones! We cannot over emphasize the importance of this practice in your own every-day living dynamics.*

A fresh new moment need be allowed to unfold as it Is, with whatever impact it may carry. ***Then, your subsequent Observation of this new moment can* nicely proceed to unfold** *without the influence of old recorded memories muddying the waters.*

Hopefully your new moment experience(s) *is now accurately recorded,* <u>devoid of corruption by judgment and opinion.</u> Your Belief System, then, can choose to lay in the fresh experience simply as an *Observation,* <u>*unblemished and as pure as your Ego will allow!*</u> *(Master chuckles .....)*

Can you see now a beautiful newly found horizon of FREEDOM knocking at your door?
The gift is yours for the taking, My Friends. I implore you to be Freedom's grateful recipient, as you receive your moments in stride with ease and grace. Many Blessings.

ॐ

Alright! I hasten to add that your examining of My six Elements to follow will serve in *sustaining* your partnership(s), as they continue to play out their various inevitable scenarios, ... certain to follow!

> *In Partnership, as in Your Own Grand Process, the middle or the end may or may not faintly resemble the beginning ... as Change has its way!*

Perhaps I have your full attention by now?

Alright. As with all of Our teachings, they are made available for the highest good of Humanity, to assist in your growth and healing.

Note well, <u>this Divine Wisdom must be allowed by you to penetrate through the armour of your Ego consciousness, whatever various levels of acceptance or resistance you have set in place</u>. This requirement is in place to allow *any* pinch of value to meld into your current life-stream …in addition to balancing Karma and healing any tears in the fabric of your Soul.

So here are the <u>Six Business Partnership Elements</u> of which I speak today:

The Glue of Formal Partnership

> **Integrity**
> **Aligned Common purpose**
> **Capability**
> **Commitment**
> **Communication**
> **Relationship**

These success-filled *Partnership Elements* provide the essential golden glue to hold the dynamics of True Partnership in place.

In every way, you are meant to be encouraged and not burdened by knowing of these fundamental essentials, either for the first time or as review! **Yes, there are** *subsets of each element***, of course.**

So Now, Dear Ones, it is <u>your job to fill in the subset blanks with the Wisdom offered unto you in this book.</u>

Congratulations will be in order as you allow these elements to inflow into your awareness.

> *Open gateways of grand opportunity, through achieving partnership pinnacles, are at your fingertips when you practice My guidance with sincerity, diligence, and openness of mind.*

Again, if you are truly sincere about your Partnership pursuits, We would direct you to reading, rereading and internalizing My written works and Spiritual Guidebooks for Mankind. They are focused upon *how to be liberated from the Human Condition* … this inborn Earthly Consciousness that deeply challenges all of You.

**I pray for your willing engagement in your process,
that this Wisdom will be your
*Guiding Mantra of Partnership Moments.***

Through Gordon Corwin II aka Lah Rahn Ananda

Chapter 4

SELF-LOVE

Your Inter-personal Relationship

"If you would be loved, love, and be loveable."
— Benjamin Franklin

A s We embrace the many parts of Relationship dynamics, a fundamental starting point and a wonderful building block to stand upon is your own Self-love.

Here is a *basis of You* as a relationship partner, and a grand part of *your own inter-personal structure of consciousness, that you yourself bring to the party, from day one!*

Surrendering to the Oneness of all life around you can ease your way along this journey of life. Spirit is ongoingly present to impassion, enliven, advise, and to vastly improve your odds of relationship success, as viewed by many various measures.

Not the least of which is this: are you showing up at the party alone, without Spirit included as a Partner or is there more? We advise that going it alone, without your Spiritual Partnership in place, deters you immeasurably and makes your Ascension journey next to impossible. **Alone** also has its extra dire consequences, <u>spanning many lifetimes turned difficult</u>, as some of you have discovered. Share in the Light and accept our helping hand and be gracious, as We are to all of you. For your own sake, regard Self-love as a magnificent and tender gift you can hold within, and radiate outwardly to others as your blessing, created in aligned Divine fashion in full Partnership with Ourselves!

Moreover, your Mastery of Self-love is intended to lead you into a deeper feeling of emotional intimacy and closeness to Oneness with the World, to your environment, and to whatever you hold most dear.

One's own *well-being* is strongly bolstered with Self-love securely nestled in place. Students of Spirit and of Human life in general are well advised to insure that Self-love energies are created of pure intent, devoid of conceit, vanity, or an *excessive regard for one's own advantage over others.*

This means, Folks, that *from the start of this party you are* **obliged** to erase any traces of 'Narcissism' that your EGO may hold sacred and/or enforce in the course of your life-stream.

Do you know that your EGO can hold you captive in it's prison if you choose to be shackled there? Are you aware *that if you allow this, Self-love shall not be yours?*

> A high ransom indeed it is, for a Human Spirit of potential to pay for the stubborn and resolute self-indulgences of Narcissism.

That said, Spirit intends that each Human engage in a sincere Self-loving process that flows in naturally as a part of **Being Human**, *without any attached sense of selfishness or guilt.* In alignment and balance, Self-love is certainly not regarded by Spirit as an obsession of Ego.

Placing the building block of Self-love in its proper slot in your belief system is meant to Be. Here is your opportunity.

Once you are clear about your Self-love and allow it to Be, you will experience a sense of inner peace that stabilizes you in the often confusing Third Dimensional world you live in, literally. Also, We mention that a greater feeling of ease is experienced by many, *as they then trust to engage deeply with Spirit, piercing the veil between worlds and communing with Ourselves on a regular basis.*

Let Us now move on to **Self-love as Part of your Personal Universe**. In Spirit, We sometimes refer to this as one *foundation segment of your Belief System*. Self-love can be portrayed in several significant and distinct parts, as you will see shown below. The refreshing part of this Belief System segment is that it can reflect *your free-will choices, blended consciously with as much honesty, authenticity with yourself, and as much TRUTH as you can muster ... all with overlapping intermingled parts, and <u>without Ego attachments</u>.*

> **Spiritual Partnership**
> **& Higher-Self Connection**

Boundaries

Needs vs. Wants.

Authentically Knowing Thyself

Self-Talk & Patience

Tuning Up Your Vibrations

Self-Nurturing and Structure

Self-Respect without EGO

Students and Chelas of Relationship evolvement need to know, once again, that this Chapter is designed to address high points of Self-love (*without your individual dramas, that could extend this transmission for eons to come!*). *We Ascended Masters observe from Above these* <u>*common*</u> *challenging threads that run through the cores of a vast number of Humans who have the admirable courage and dedication to pursue an examined lifetime.*

'*Self-love leads you to find peace within yourself.*

Amen'.

ॐ ॐ

Spiritual Partnership and Your Higher-Self Connection

"*Gaining awareness is the first step in your liberation from the Human Illusion*"

Lord Saint Germain 08-16-16

In this incarnation, one of the grandest challenges you face is to get out of your own way and let the Light shine in to your own Being. During this process, your belief system needs to let go of preconceived notions that would *separate you from Being the real and <u>authentic you</u> that enthusiastically embraces Self-love and Spirit as a Partner.*

The intention of this Chapter is to light up the Self-loving part of your Spiritual path. *Along this way, with some heartfelt diligence and aligned engagement of mind, body and Soul, you can harness and apply Practical Spirituality in loving yourself to the fullest, without the tethers that Ego would otherwise bind you to the Human Illusion. Are you following me so far?*

In these sections embracing Self-love, please for your own sake, *take notice of key areas and ingredients that we will be discussing: Order, Love, Truth, Patience, Courage, Clarity, Needs and Wants, Awareness, Boundaries, Upsets, Emotions, Self-talk, Higher Self, Patience, Forgiveness, Aligned Action, Self-respect, Tuning up your Vibrations and Self-monitoring, among others.*

As these essentials for your evolution of consciousness are *carefully unwound, distinct from ordinary Human life chaos, you will be given insights and invitations to willingly blend these key ingredients (and more) into the mix, laying them in place in an orderly fashion, guiding you along an otherwise route of 'Ego stumbling' on your own.*

Do yourself a favor and reread the above paragraph about 'Going it Alone'.

With fundamental building blocks in place, We offer the opportunity to encapsulate for yourself certain *gifts of guidance that will serve you well in conquering this part of the Human Illusion.* In concert with this process, you may receive *revelations in connecting at a deeper level to your Higher-Self. So B*e open and aware of what your process has in store for you as it unfolds, day by day! This phase of personal relationships is heart-warming to say the least ... let it freely nourish the tendrils of your heart and Soul!

In the Self-Love Circle shown above, notice We *start at the top with your Spiritual Partnership and your Higher-Self connection, a relationship of Love.*

From

△ The Ultimate Love Triangle △

Lords Jesus Ananda and Saint Germain together as One.

Through Lah Rahn Ananda aka Gordon Corwin II

Published prior: www.SaintGermainChronicles.com 2018

About Love

Love is a wondrous special space you can truly enter into and dwell within, gifted as a quintessential part of your Personal Universe. In the beginning, the essence of Love itself was planted and deeply rooted as part of your Human core Being. As you so evolve in this lifetime, your aura can include this tender space, *held in your consciousness in varying intensities, higher vibrational spaces you sustain or enter from time to time, if that be your level of Love evolvement.*

And, where Love is yearned for, perhaps it magically appears for you as a place you have longed to enter and wonder why it has evaded you … and here it is?

We come to you today, as in each Earth day, as two of many Ascended Brothers, All joined as One. In these transmissions, it is good to know you are well-served and Blessed with our energies that emanate directly from the Divine Mind of God. We are Divine Emissaries. In the essence of Love, Purity and Freedom abound, apart from contorted Earthly or outside interferences. In these transmissions, our surrendered Instrument on Earth is serving you at our request, transmuting Our Divine ethereal energies into Human Language. Masterful Wisdom then becomes available for you to integrate into your consciousness, *a Blessing for on-going use in your daily life.* Lord Jesus, Lah Rahn Ananda, and I, as Lord Saint Germain, serve together, dedicated to the Spiritual Enlightenment of Humanity. Come and join us!

Developing your own gift of accessing Spirit will evolve over time, as abilities are incubated, born, deserved, and then honed under our guiding hands. Increased listening to voices of Ascended Masters is a gradual process, beginning with hatching aligned intuitions, and hearing bits and bytes from Above. *Let Patience be your Friend!*

So what about 'my' emotions, you ask? The process of transcending *your* own flood of incoming emotions can indeed pose challenging obstacles, We realize this. And yet, *conscious attention to following our guidance about purifying your process will truly lead you past these distractions. Note:* Chapter 8 to follow in sequence is entitled Emotions!

Know that your Soul yearns to activate this *refined form of pure consciousness* embodying Love throughout each of your lifetimes. Here and now is your opening in hand!! Here lies another beauteous opportunity in a surrendered Human lifetime, to deeply engage … into a Love space of ease and grace, joy, and enjoyment … where you can grow to dwell, and be overshined with Light during all of your moments of daily living. Blessings.

◆ ◆

Authentically Knowing Thyself

As Ones come closer to Spirit and greater Self-Love, We see a beautiful surrendering of old patterns in favor of *being honest with yourself*. Fooling others? Sometimes, and perhaps not, as *you know the truth of you inside your core.*

'Being Truth is Self-Love".

Self-discovery of your *default* patterns of action, thought, and emotional behavior is fascinating when you finally see, … 'ahhh haa, … I'm not who I said I was earlier on … I am re-discovering myself … I Am moving my vibration to a higher level!' I am learning about *little secrets!*

- Exactly what are my little secrets, that make up this formerly hidden part of my Being?

- What do I do when no one is watching?

- What do I do when I think I won't get caught?

- Am I willing to set up <u>new default patterns</u> of pause, contemplation, and patience before I respond?

- What do I do when I don't get what I want? (*that's a big one Folks*).

- What are my triggers that make me react? KNOWING the answers to these questions and then applying them to your life makes a humongous difference for you to reshape your character to meet a higher vibration … <u>going from who you are now to who you choose to be in Relationships from now on!</u>

Here lies a <u>**beginning process of living an extraordinary and fully examined lifetime, one that is worth living!**</u> Self-discovery is a fascinating undertaking when you penetrate below your own surface veneer layer of appearances and truly know yourself.

> *Truly and fully knowing yourself disarms self-deception and denial, Folks. Fooling One's self (remember Spirit and the Lords of Karma are watching) is the oldest racket on your Planet, and unintended transparency often gives away your secrecy as part of your self-deception.*

Finding and knowing your own trigger points, default responses, and knee jerk responses when stressed, for example, is another dimension of knowing yourself, a discussion Chapter you will later read in this book.

Be amazed at what you uncover, Dear Ones, when you are honestly introspective and *get into the bottom layers with authenticity. Don't be tempted to employ your denial strategies, 'oh that does not apply to me' approach, because fooling yourself has great consequences later on. It keeps you stuck!*

You are encouraged to give this Knowing Yourself process your very all ... to <u>Authentically Know Yourself,</u> and to consult with *Ourselves* for insights and revelations, which are abundant for aware listeners of Spirit's signs, messages, gifts of synchronicity and Our transmissions, of course. WE never sleep!

Needs versus Wants

Relationship partners of various types are often called upon to wisely make known their *Needs and Wants.* While very often confusing the two, some <u>Priorities</u> can be nicely set in place and effectively carried out *when the relationship itself is crystal clear about these two distinctions,* ... Wants and Needs are distinctly different! And, sometimes there are instances where both are *tied together in harmony,* (isn't that ironic?) Is the mystery of irony peeking out here a bit as in other parts of this book?

Dealing effectively with your own Needs versus Wants requires a conscious clarity *and* a setting of priorities to respect the difference!

When Needs are given priority, the partners can *individually or together* give priority emphasis to obligations that are urgently present, past, waiting, or lingering in the wings of the future.

Also, along with relationship needs, is it not true that *individual partners* also have needs? *Others in the relationship would be wise to acknowledge this, and consciously treat these needs with care, compassion, and respect! Are partners not all on the same team?*

> *Notice the sense of Freedom that you can generate when there is clarity about handling a need in an effective way, ... at the ideal time ... with priority that fits the need!*

Wants. *Knowing that <u>you</u> can put aside your own purely selfish motivations of <u>wants</u> in favor of lovingly honoring legitimate <u>needs</u> of a relationship or a relationship partner, can bring enormous gratification and <u>strength to your own Self-love!</u> <u>And to the relationship itself as well, yes?</u>*

When Wants show up, relationship partners *also have a clear-cut responsibility <u>to be able to recognize a Want</u>, and give it the priority it deserves as a Want, while respecting other Wants and those <u>higher priority</u> Needs that may be on the table!*

Notice how 'Teamwork' can be wondrous in this

interplay (that also tests the <u>shared control</u> in your relationship).

> This practice of Wants and Needs distinctions, having clarity, and setting priorities accordingly may seem elementary. We see this as a 'taken for granted approach' by the unaware, who remain confused and content in their ignorant and intransigent stance! We see this lack of clarity as a major stumbling block for partners in relationship, believe it or not! The wise will insure that this practice of distinction is now tattooed in their consciousness(es) and in their prefrontal cache memories for fast random access, as you say!

So for yourself, here is an opportunity to dive in. List for your own life the **Needs vs. Priority Wants** that you are working with:

NEEDS   WANTS

_____
_____
_____
_____
_____
_____
_____
_____
_____
_____
_____

When *this distinction* process becomes a routine part of you... and for <u>ALL partners working willingly and agreeably in unison</u>, you ALL will notice the magical harmonies and synchronicities that the Universe can bring!

Boundaries

Let us look now at Boundaries from a personal perspective ... that of a relationship partner, ... individually as a part of Self-love.

Personal Universe boundaries vary so greatly, that here <u>We can simply suggest some sample parameters that may shed light on your own unique makeup of consciousness.</u>

In the arena of Personal Boundaries, *some are absolute and unnegotiable, while some are less rigid, with perhaps a little wiggle room.*

Let Me now briefly state a paramount, gigantic point of Truth, enabling you to elevate and sustain your Relationships of all types. Alright! *Your ultimate success in creating and sustaining loving, Self-loving, and satisfying Relationships depends greatly upon your Free-will Choices to adequately blend the Boundaries of your consciousness!*

There is a *delicate balance* in play here, to respect the boundary itself, and yet to simultaneously *blend and perhaps soften* that boundary a bit in the process! From the below diagram, focus for now upon the ME and WE boundaries, and visualize how you can adequately balance and connect these energies into Oneness ... in place of *abrupt separation*. This Balance is yours to create, Dear Ones!

This pictorial overlap of consciousnesses shows a synchronous blending of energies that is needed for a true relationship to be born, blossom, and thrive.

Blending of Consciousness

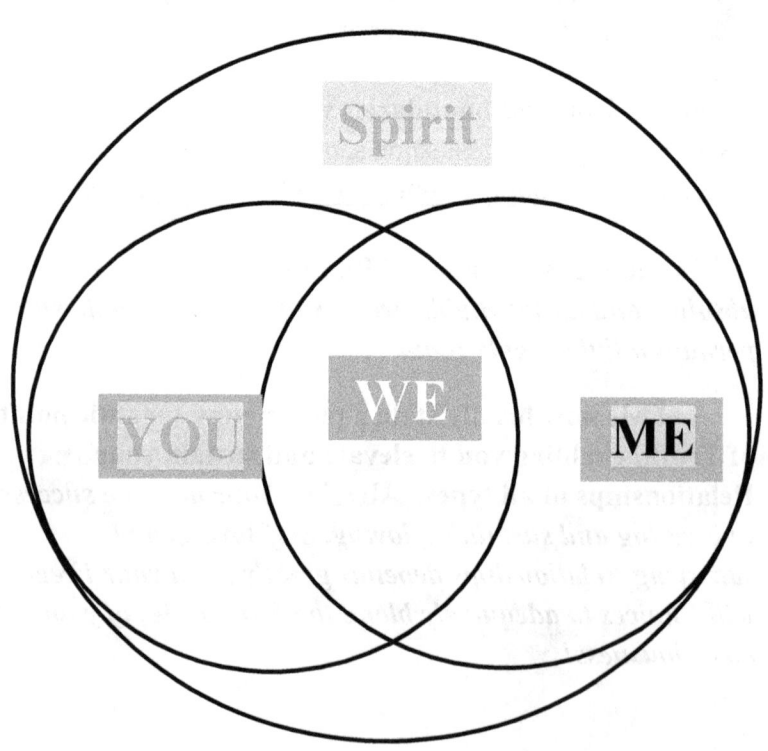

Your own Boundaries, some as absolute and some as negotiable (you can list for yourself below), could include areas of: *nurturing, control, being appropriately respected, integrity, honesty, trustworthiness, unwavering responsibility, satisfaction, courtesy, love, kindness, discipline, timeliness, communications, responsiveness, recognition of others, .….*

… the list below is yours to create, sort out, and write. Take your time here, as this part defines in a large way <u>who you really are in this respect about your Boundaries!</u> <u>Note that they may well change as your relationship progresses.</u>

My Boundaries	**Date**

Freely update this Boundary list, as it will inevitably change as you evolve. Be patient with yourself, and look deeply into your inner planes of Being. This may take some meditation and cogitation before the list is complete. Beware to keep your Ego out of the way! This is only one piece of the puzzle, my Good Friends! Good tidings!

Other key ingredients to the wholeness of SELF-LOVE: 'Self-Talk' and 'Patience', ... both, ... are spoken of at great length in *separate Chapters of this book*, to duly emphasize their extreme importance in your relationship training.

Alright!
Self-Love is also <u>to open a new pattern and pathway for yourself</u>, *abandoning the EGO's firm grip and stance of supremacy. Without an Ego that is in charge, believe it or not at this point, the effects of upset can noticeably subside and can soon vanish into the Ethers, as We Masters will answer aligned requests to take distress from you.*

Authentically summoning pure COURAGE is also a part of Self-love. This could include requests to Ourselves for guidance. Yes, upon legitimate request, We are known to assist! Have you asked lately?

NEW PERSPECTIVES. We teach students of Spirit, Truth seekers, Light Carriers ... all ... to seek out NEW PERSPECTIVES as *they <u>contemplate</u> and <u>observe</u> Earthly events, circumstances, emotions, and interactions of relationship that penetrate a life-stream and give cause for questioning.*

As you contemplate perspectives, *have you ever considered Lord Chief Joseph's sage advice to <u>"stand in the other man's shoes, feel what he may be feeling, and look back at yourself, standing in your own shoes"</u>? Try it sometime! Let Me know how it works out for you!*

Many find that this standing in the other man's shoes process *opens many portals, some of which are internal to the examiners own heart chakra energies that may need to be cleared. Once fully cleared at the heart level, new perspectives and solutions are known to joyfully pop up in a spontaneous and magical time of new inspiration.*

Backing off from the magnifying glass approach, *where little details can cloud the issue, and standing where you can see the BIG PICTURE will enormously assist your EGO in surrendering to achieve your Upset completions and restore you to the highest level of vibration you can muster at this level of evolvement.*

Self-love compassion can also free you a bit here, knowing that some of these upset circumstances are part of being Human and out of your CONTROL!
Allow for yourself some adapting and regrouping, flowing with the new energy you <u>bring into the situation</u>, and simply surrendering to 'what is'. As you LET GO, miracles can use the space within that you allow to work for you.

Self-talk. WE pray you have now learned or relearned the tremendous power of aligned and constructive, and positive Self-talk that truly supports your Self-love. Attention need be given to your own Self-talk on a daily, hourly, and sometimes momentary basis, as it can easily slip into disempowering unwanted territory.

Listen carefully to yourself, Folks! You would be amazed at the Human Self-talk We hear in the Ethers! Oh My! And the differences between certain individual's Self-talk and *what they actually talk aloud*! This takes Us into authenticity and hypocrisy, My friends, a topic which We will later address.

Peace of mind? Do yourself a huge favor and lift yourself up with self-inspiring mind talk that comes from the best parts of you. Aummmmm.

Decrees are available as a bridge to refocus your Self-talk when need be.

❧

Self-nurturing and Structure

Every person in a Relationship has a **Divine Obligation** to honor themselves, mind, body, and Higher-self. These are your sacred temples in which you dwell as an incarnated Human.

Structuring a self-nurturing routine for your daily life is an admirable feat in these rush-rush times of immense competition for Your time! Set aside some self-nurturing time, just for you! You are worthy of this!

And also appropriate amounts of self-nurturing time, some devoted each day, and some particular day of the week during which you can UNWIND your nerves, settle in, and receive some satisfying stimuli that relaxes and heals you. It's an essential healing ingredient of Self-love, good People!

Beyond just self-preservation, think of the myriads of self-nurturing choices you have at your fingertips. We know about the explosion of vast choices now available!

Research well, as you will, and choose wisely, ... this is a personal matter. **Listening to your body** is a great place to start, and *answering bodily needs and certain wants with self-loving care is part of the job. Many of You are learning to listen to your bodies more and more, as* <u>*health-responsible Ones*</u> *gain in numbers. Did you know that many of you actually have to* <u>*give yourself permission*</u> *to be self-nourished? We caution against overindulgence and obsession, of course, as many who lack temperance will fall into this trap.*

Similarly, your mind and consciousness can be nurtured with **transcendental meditation**, perhaps with flowers, candles, and incense, or with the company of empowering friends and groups, the saying of Decrees, ... and reading this and other books like this!

Self-talk, discussed in another chapter in great detail, can powerfully complement your self-nourishing when structured with positive energies of Truth and Love.

On a physical level, We notice Humans could benefit with getting *sufficient sleep and regular exercise,* time honored healing modalities commonly ignored by Humankind as We observe. Could you look in your mirror and find a wake-up call?

Your daily routine can be *structured* to support your overall well-being ... a routine to include some or all of the above nurturing activities. Beyond taking care of Wants and Needs, how about working into your schedule some *planned recreation.*

We support all relationships to form a mutually supportive structure, especially in the inspiration phase of a beginning Relationship. Elements here could include mutual promises to positively support each other, being fair and up front with feelings you express to a partner, having compassion for all needs and wants as you present your case with the highest vibrations you can muster, with a willingness to also stare reality in the face!

Practice makes perfect Mastery of this process, and discovering a structure that works for you will require ongoing discipline, as you have probably sensed by now.

Self-love embraces *treating yourself* in a loving way that supports your life purpose, develops and manifests your potentials, and shows due consideration for others well-being. Blending the harmony of 'I' and 'We' is a wonderful space to occupy as you respect your Self-love without Ego.

Self-respect without Ego

This is perhaps one of the grandest opportunities and most daunting challenges, all wrapped together! A true Self-respect without Ego embodies a consciousness of Self-love that holds a humble and favorable esteem, while free of egotistical or narcissistic values.

The fact that you concentrate and imbed Self-love, without selfishness into your Being is in itself Self-Respect without Ego!

Here I ask you to note well a behavior most obvious in your World of Corona Chaos at the time of this writing. Note how many of your *world leaders, as wells as individuals in the rank and file, are <u>inexorably obsessed with pleasing their EGO DEMANDS! So much so that they are literally willing to deliberately and arrogantly risk their very lives (and the lives of a nation) to satisfy these EGO demands, devoid of Self-respect and Self-Love.</u> These choices clearly block progress toward higher solutions opting for a behavior that promotes the highest good of Humanity and the Earth World! Many such Ego-infested Ones, including some in possession of great Earthly power, are on a collision course with themselves! We pray this does not include you, whatever be your role in Human life, this time around!*

<u>This collective test for Humanity, ... and for you as an individual, ... now looks you squarely in the face.</u> You have the tools for self-preservation and happiness in a continuing life stream, IF you remain awake and make your wise and aligned choices ... day by day! I encourage you to stay alert and to Be the Self-Love that is your birth right!

With conscious devotion, discipline, and self-care, your Personal Universe can be tailored to nicely include Self-respect along with Self-Love, ... embedded with honesty and authenticity, ... securely holding within as much TRUTH as you can muster. All of this may be nicely mixed together *with overlapping layers of consciousness,* ... without succumbing to Ego attachments when they may attempt to grab you. ***To be clear and to the point, 'being right' is not a fundamental of Self-respect or Self-Love, Folks, … it is a pillar of Ego! This Truth will shock those of you inextricably trapped in the Human Illusion. Does the shoe fit?***

Below you will see:

Tuning Up
Your Vibrations

A page to follow will give you some random examples of Ego Behavior that We see as prevalent. *This is by no means an exhaustive list*, which would require more pages than this book could hold, I hasten to add!

Notice that the Highest-Self Choices focus upon alternative behaviors that connect with Spirit, leading to Truth rather than escalating into further ego extensions.

When a Student of Spirit encounters an explosive situation, laced with observed Ego behaviors such as shown below, often times a *request can be made 'would you mind rephrasing that in another way please?'* A speaker or writer can then be given the invitation to raise the vibration of their stance, **opening the way to a possible Win-Win solution.**

Tuning up Your Vibrations
~ Applied Spirituality from Saint Germain ~

EGO Behavior *compared with* ## Your Highest-Self Choices

"My small story is what counts!" Over dramatizes. Is selfishly focused, ignoring Unity consciousness.

Ego confuses its small story with Reality! Indulges in *fear-based behavior*, including anger.

Strives to be "important". The BIG shot! Greedy!

Overcomes EGO's burning indulgence.
Replaced with *aligned self-choices for highest good.*
Learns, applies, and remembers life's lessons. Embraces this process with empathy and overshining fear of change.
Knows Joy through *humility* and helpfulness.

"I'm always right" attitude. Arrogant. Believes Ego's *opinion* is correct! Ignores Human fallibility. Re-enforces a sagging self-esteem by denial.

Seeks Truth, applying the merit of different perspectives to each moment of every day life.
Replaces denial with reality and self-integrity!

My opinion, i.e., "*my* truth", IS *the* Truth!!! "There are no other possibilities but mine!"

Discerns the *difference* between their belief system and *Universal law / Truth.*

Self-Aggrandizes. *Dominates* selfishly to over-ride or restrict others' Free-will choices. Makes untenable excuses. Projects the blame onto another one/thing. "It's someone else's fault". *Avoids accountability and responsibility.*

Seeks Mastery of Spirit's teachings of Truth. See The Saint Germain Chroniclers Collection.
Knows Truth and accepts reality with Joy.
Pacifies an untamed EGO into submission into its rightful role. Promotes harmony.

Complains about *unfulfilled expectations.* Demands *immediate* satisfaction! Prefers *complaining* to implementing solutions!
Gets "stuck" on irreconcilable issues

Demonstrates patience by shrinking EGO's stature, now relegated *to take a back seat.*

Obsesses about dissatisfactions.

Seeks out and implements creative Win-win solutions.
Replaces complaints without squandering energy.
Expresses gratefulness. Sees Blessings!

Escalates frustration into anger and hate. Enjoys being angry; regards as acceptable! *Impatience* accelerates into anger.
Believes anger or hate get the best results,

Utilizes Saint Germain's
healing techniques as presented in His book 'Victory for the Soul, Relationships That Work',
Gordon Corwin II -Lah Rahn Ananda, Amazon.

Uses anger to "bully" others, often hiding *fear*. Promotes conflict and greed. Seeks revenge. Unable and or unwilling to *recognize emotions.*

Recognizes *own* behavior in real-time.
Elevates negative emotions, raising them up into
Neutral or Positive zones.
Is accountable for Own Behaviors.

Satisfied staying stuck in Egos's versions
of unlearned life's lessons.

Attached to Ego as a prisoner of its own device.

Fully ENJOYS the Mastery and rewards of Aligned Actions and Higher Dimensions. Discovers the Human Condition! Transcends the Human Illusion!!

Aligns consciousness with Universal / Divine Law, *freeing their Highest-Self to BE.*

"To Truly Be or not to BE is Your Question". Saint Germain
Through Lah Rahn Ananda 05/2010 Rev. 07/2022

Chapter 5

PATIENCE

"If a string is in a knot,
Patience will untie it.
Patience can do many things -
did you ever try it?"

Anna M. Pratt

A common denominator running through all *flourishing relationships*, personal, interpersonal, and associative, is the quality of patience, viscerally laced into One's highest character.

Seemingly obvious and yet often overlooked in relationships, is the immense importance of personally practicing patience ongoingly, … a gigantic contribution from you to you … to act *as a catalyst to enhance your abilities to Master Self-love, change, communication, emotions, forgiveness, and a host of other behavioral qualities imbedded in "Victory For The Soul, Relationships That Work".*

Patience itself has been long stated as a virtue of character, and although this be true, relationships can hinge on actually <u>practicing</u> *this virtuous quality … in action,* especially when learning curves come to the forefront and call for needed changes!

Speaking for a moment as the Author, *I have observed over many years, certain fortunate individuals who seem to have an inborn quality of patience that is natural, effortless, and often included in their lifestyle and behaviors, even when emotional! These types are Blessed to have relationships that can often flourish, often with ease and grace! It is heartwarming to observe these individuals, sometimes as magnets of mysterious attraction.*

And, on the flip side as polar opposites, I have also been exposed to those with short fuses in almost every part of their lives, with no shred of evidence of patience in their character or behaviors, and with a glaring abundance of Ego in action, front and center! These types will often explode at the slightest provocation, with no evidence of patience anywhere to be seen! Maybe you have noticed? Saint Germain's teachings show that rewards of patience are countless when we are aware, awake, and teachable. Over the Ages, Masters have said that a great reward from practicing patience is ... more patience. Lah Rahn

𝔖aint 𝔊ermain continues:

In any case, We must address this topic separately, as its own Chapter, to give those Ones in need of patience the attention that *patience deserves and commands.* By practice, conscious attention, and perseverance, your application of patience in making choices, responses, decisions, etc. can become an invaluable <u>learned behavior</u>, <u>an *enduring habit that will constructively support every phase of your life!*</u>

From a higher vibrational standpoint, you may have noticed the presence of 'Divine Timing' in your own individual lives and particularly in relationships, of which We now speak.

Divine Timing is a mysterious, usually non-understandable, mind boggling, magical feat of the Universe. *Here, contrary to Ego wants and illusionary needs, aligned and worthy requests are fulfilled by Spirit in Divine time. The manifestation timing of outcomes and events seem to **occur out of nowhere** and at a set time and date orchestrated by Spirit, mindboggling as this may seem. The arrival of a Divinely Timed synchronicity outcome is commonly a surprise, sometimes earlier and sometimes later than a person may wish or request, directly or in prayer. Patience is required for you to be the benefactor of such Divine Timing outcomes, ... if you choose to be on-board?*

> The point here is that Patience is needed for Divine Timing to incubate and then have its way, beneficially flowing into your life-stream.

The Mystery of Spirit needs to be simply embraced and 'known' by your Loving-Self, rather than mentally sought after as a 'thing' to be understood or chased after. This is a fundamental Spiritual axiom. Oh, how many have traveled this road of demanding only to understand and ended up stuck with their chariot wheel in a wagon rut, never to be extricated ... or should We say exhumed, in this lifetime? *Is it a difference between understanding escalated into Knowing or Being? Certainly so!*

Patience and Divine Timing. Strangely enough, (and your intuition can guide you), only *certain life's events are candidates for Divine Timing. Your tests are to show and demonstrate the patience required to then let Divine Timing manifest, if it shall, in Divine alignment and Divine Order. Part of your journey is to sense and follow Spirit's guidance, with a learned awareness and without Ego interference, when opportunities are open for you.*

Accessing the Universe of Attraction. There is a basic *choice* that surfaces about patience. You can live your life in scarcity and fear, and rely on your Ego to fulfill your wants and needs. Or, in Spiritual Partnership, you can align with the Source, *have patience*, and manifest in this Partnership what is next in your life's path and Soul's blueprint.

❧❦

Patience with Change itself

Much has been said about Change in this Book, and more shall be said. **To invoke ease and grace into One's life, a lasting adaptability to Change requires patience, … a requirement often compounded when you are in limbo about all the facts or the outcome of a circumstance.** In some cases, analogous to 'waiting for your turn' perhaps?

Yes, surely Change is surrounding you upon all sides as you are experiencing and deeply feeling in your chaotic

Earth-world. *Your meditation practice* is highly recommended to assist you at this time and always. Your meditation must continue! A quiet mind will allow adaptation which may otherwise elude when change is knocking at your door.

❧☙

Patience in your Communications

The ease and grace of interacting in Relationship is so greatly benefited by *clear, smooth, and timely communication between partners. Your attention to these qualities will bring bountiful rewards if you have the <u>patience</u> and <u>perseverance</u> to put them into actual practice!* Countless speedbumps and tangles are thereby avoided and eliminated, nipped in the bud, often before they escalate. Treat yourselves to this Blessing, My Dear Ones.

Slow down, and give your communications the *patient* ***TLC*** *and clarity, and heartfulness they deserve. Communications form a wonderfully important part of any relationship, and slowing down as you communicate may require <u>a little extra patience from all partners</u>.* Remember, rushing the process can have its consequences, Folks!

Speaking as the Author, ... traveling on a long awaited fly-fishing trip, ... I once heard an old Bahamian fisherman exclaim a saying to me. He spoke when I was searching and struggling for patience to catch an elusive bonefish in the Caribbean ocean waters: *"Patience Gordy, if you rush the brush, you smear the paint"*.
I am forever indebted to this man for the stark wisdom in the moment ... and for finally catching <u>and</u> releasing the fish!

❦

Patience in Decision Making

Have you ever patiently considered *pondering* an important decision and action that needs attention, and then decided to sleep on it for a night or two before firming it up?

Upcoming generations, We observe, seem to rush their speaking, at times to the point of incoherence, to fit the peer pressured mold they value so highly. Talking fast and using incomplete sentences and thoughts, often **digital in nature,** has become a *behavioral standard of certain generations upcoming on your Earth plane.*

Have you noticed these impatient communication inadequacies and breakdowns that result? Have you considered framing your speaking or writing in ways that can be heard and understood?
Effective language *is available* at your fingertips and the tips of your tongues, if you have the strength of character and skill to Master and use it to the fullest!

"Genius is nothing but a greater aptitude for patience."
— Benjamin Franklin

Patience with Temptations of Ego

Patience is a partially learned skill and partially inborn in some cases. To attain a state of higher vibration, and then <u>maintain</u> it, even when tempting emotions pull One off track, patience is required at ALL times, ... <u>**not just when your convenience dictates!**</u>

In a State of Reacting, where Ego takes over, and *higher consciousness is immobilized,* frozen, and overshadowed, often by default Ego reactions, patience has little opportunity to bring clarity … meaning that the power of your Spirit is compromised! <u>Losing One's temper gives away your Spiritual Power and your ability to use your gifts!   Recognize and learn this behavior, and your life will change!</u>

> *Patience is the catalyst that allows space for creation of solutions!*

Ranting, rage, anger, and hate all drag a high vibrating Being down into the depths where little is accomplished, save perhaps Ego satisfaction with *emotional release outbursts.*

T reat yourself to read elsewhere in this Book about the *discipline* of avoiding anger and avoiding judgments as you master patience.

Patience opens space for the solution to emerge, *be introduced into the interaction! Notice the difference between a mere compromise and a true Win-Win solution, hatched with patience and insights of new perspectives. By nature, a <u>compromise</u> is often used as a solution to resolve conflicting wants or needs, giving each party what it can* *tolerate and 'live with', but not all they necessarily want or need, and the same for the other party.*

In a compromise, a mixture of satisfaction and dissatisfaction can result. <u>Adding competition</u> in this interaction further complicates arriving at a solution with the introduction of this age old Earthly practice of Human Beings ... trapped into the 3rd Dimension of Consciousness.

⊗   I Win   —   You Lose

The mindset of "I Win - You Lose" is an old time favorite default Ego strategy... it is an iron-clad pillar of 3rd Dimensional Ego behavior. Sad but true. Look around you, Good People!

Does this ring a bell with you? <u>We are speaking of Separation.</u> **See for yourself how much of your Earth-plane mindset is infested with this collapsed competitive and separatist vibration as common behavior?**

Can this awareness be a major change and turning point for you? We shall see!

We are speaking about Separation. How much of your Duality on the Earth Plane is infested with this collapsed competitive and separatist vibration?

Domination

In conjunction with the Ego infested 'I Win and You lose mindset', We need, at this point, to mention a connection with the <u>force of Domination</u>. *This Ego driven behavior, sometimes wildly obsessive, is a forceful desire and illusionary need to control. As you would say, 'my way or the highway'? We see from Above Human behaviors of domination are largely fear driven, ironically ... with an underlying insecurity linked to survival.*

In relationships freely flowing in love and co-operation, ... and patience ... this domination mindset is easily transcended and transmuted into the grace of Us and We, blending together with ease and <u>shared control in place</u>. Re-read this paragraph Dear Ones, ... it will save you when you need it most!

Patience in Dealing with the Earthly Duality

On the Earth Plane, patience is indeed commendable for Humans that can muster the gumption! The choice between dark and light in the Earthly Duality presents Humanity with monstrous dilemmas, perhaps the most obvious being that of COMPETITION. Does this resonate with you in any way? <u>If One looks objectively at Duality, *separation* is its true name.</u>

And if you have a burning desire to delve into the dynamics of Earthly Human competition, let patience be with you as you wait to read My CHAPTER 20 which lies ahead for you in this book!

Meanwhile, can you see the man-made behavior pattern of competition? Can you see how it is a <u>man-made behavorial tradition of Duality</u>, <u>based on Ego, fear and survival?</u>

Notice how the collective of Humanity has morphed into a mode of competition housed in Duality? Ponder this if you will! Ponder *the far reaching tentacles* of competition, in your businesses, careers, money, sporting events, on and on!

As We dwell Above, We act in the unison of Oneness, since Ego and underlying judgment has been altogether purified here in the Ethers and completely washed away from the Ascended collective consciousness. Competition does not exist Above. There is no Win-lose mentality in Our energy fields.

Let this be your goal, as you too climb the Spiritual ladder of Ascension, rung by rung *with patience.*

We, as Ascended Masters, are composed of the Divine mind. We have All accessed the ability to transcend the collective of your Earth Duality. We intend to substitute Our Divine Mindset upon Earth such that you create solutions, in place of Humanity's Win-lose favorite behavior. The parties involved all get 'what they want', emerging happy and fulfilled and devoid of Separation!

You are wise to emulate the Divine Mind at every opportunity, day by day! We support you in your continuing efforts, challenging as that may be, to embrace patience as your forever friend and ally.

"He that can have patience can have what he will"
Benjamin Franklin

"The Hardest test in life is the

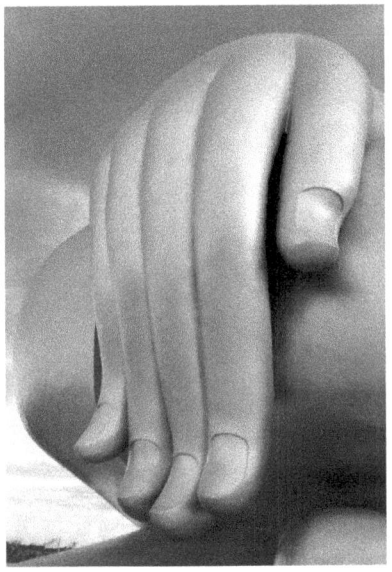

Patience to wait for the right *Moment*"

Buddha

Picture - Golden Hand of the Giant Buddha

Chapter 6

SELF-TALK
Internal conversations between many parts within you.

We have much to say about this component of Self-talk, so hang on to thy hat!

Self-talk is the private conversation you have within *the ALL of you*. Realize that talking to One's self can intermingle a mixture of inputs from your entire belief system. As you read on, study the consciousness perspectives diagram to follow.

Your own Contributors to this conversation may include your intuition, your Ego, Higher-self, life experiences, life lessons, belief system, judgments, opinions and more. We would empower you to *let your Higher-self be in charge, as the internal referee between these sometimes conflicting perspectives within you, And, of course, to be Divinely coached by Spirit.*

Have you felt your own various voices from within sometimes compete, yes? We guide you to let your Ego have last place in the lineup of voices to be obeyed.

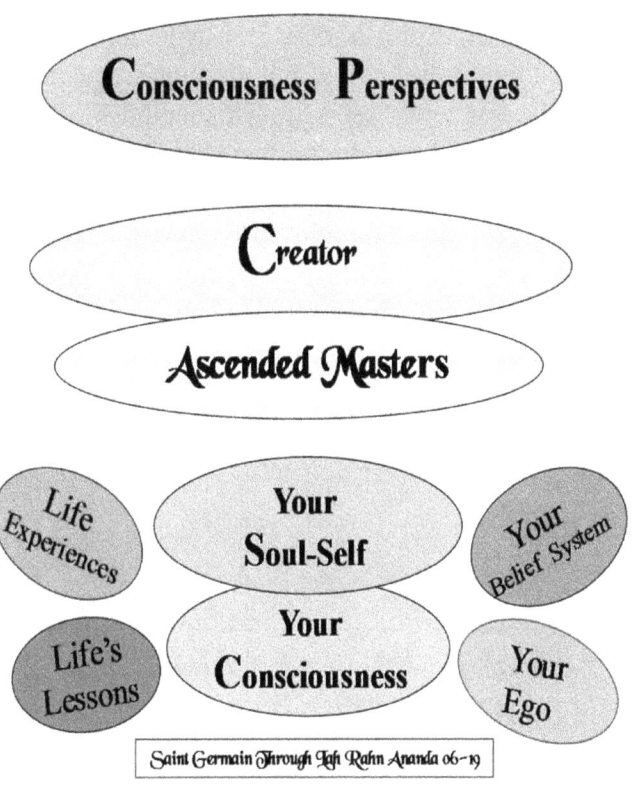

Be aware that You and you alone control the nature of your Self-talk. Spirit honors Free-will choice as Humans walk their life paths, <u>and no interference from Above is allowed with Free-will</u>. This includes *your choice*s of Self-talk! Mastering your Free-will choices, thought by thought, is a vital part of your Spiritual Journey, Folks. Let Us say it is a delightful freedom that comes with great concurrent responsibility ... distinct and specific to Humankind among many Cosmic species seeking enlightenment! You are special in this way!

Ones who are aware, positive, and Spiritually uplifted, will source their Self-talk for the highest good of All.

> <u>A Healthy Self-talk dialogue</u> can sing delightfully to the highest octave of your consciousness and make you smile, inside and out!

In a sense, your Self-talk defines a large part of who you really are as a ***Being at the core level.***

Self-talk influences all phases of your life, and has no bounds, save the ones that you impose. When it is self-supporting, We are speaking about a habitual way of Being that nourishes your thinking, speaking, choices, general and specific outlooks, *and the very use of your belief system.*

We are referring to a *habitual way of Being* that reflects your choice of how you shall BE!

Joy and Freedom can be so powerfully included in your Self-talk that you breeze through your emotional ups and downs with an ease and grace. Ironically, this defaults into a higher state of vibration ... free from much Human illusion.

> *Inner peace, as you may discover, is directly related to the quality of your own Self-talk. This is Happiness you yourself find, nourish, and hold within, when you are on top of your game.*

We acknowledge that Self-talk co-exists alongside outer Earthly chatter as well, simultaneously mixed with these transient energies. Your job is to sort it out!
And then there is your *inner Self-talk* distinct from that talk that you release *outside of yourself to others.*

- Now, observe if you will, how *different* your inner Self-talk may be from the words you say in your outer speaking. Be careful here! Your *authenticity* may be at stake! **"Outside talk" can often be justly accused of hypocrisy when compared to "Inside Self-talk". Do you see?**

At this beginning, We again emphasize PATIENCE *as a quintessential* ingredient in this Self-talk treatise, as it deeply affects your Self-love dynamics. *Be kind to yourself and hold your Self-talk, Self-love and Patience allies near to your heart, forever and ever.*
These are visceral parts of you ... parts to be highly prized! If you are wise, you will keep these intact at all times, ... as this trio is yours to own and cherish without permissions from your relationship partner(s). It belongs to you alone. It can be a bountiful gift from **yourself to yourself.**

As you remember, We have created for you an entire preceding Chapter in this book entitled *PATIENCE.*
To integrate fully with your Self-talk ... kindly re-read and intake the *patience wisdom* with great care throughout your reading, as you absorb and apply relationship guidance to follow.

A grand peacemaker within you *is using your ability to self-acknowledge* <u>*without Ego*</u> *when you have done your very personal best! In Self-talk, ... 'I know I have just done my personal best Lord, 110% or more, and I AM at peace in this moment. I ask for Your Blessing. I AM willing to create tomorrow to be even better'.*

In guiding you, **We will often point out that your Self-talk will, in fact, <u>need periodic positive correction</u>. It will need a nudge to change course. The course itself is <u>your</u> choice!**

As each day progresses, take the time to love yourself by observing *the <u>tenor of your Self-talk</u>* **in your moments.** *Is it open and positive, eager and ready to pluck ripe moments from the vine, those voices of opportunity and higher vibrational nature? Or is it handcuffing you by being emotionally reactive, grumpy, negative, suspicious, judgmental, self-defeating and squawking at other lower vibrational levels?*

<u>**A focused, productively occupied mind**</u> *set can nicely attend to the tasks at hand, incorporating Self-talk to support the successful outcome of that task. Others can also support you as they would sense your Self-talk, but remember, your 'Self-talk' is solo, masked to most others perceptions.*

We see Self-talk intruding on a consciousness, both when the mind is occupied, and then when it is unoccupied, … as in 'idle'.

An idle mind, *like a parked car, engine running and sitting ready in gear, presents a different picture! The idle mind presents an <u>open target for the Ego</u>, and your own other contributors, as mentioned above, <u>to have their say, and to have their way with YOU.</u>*

Oftentimes, We see an emotional battle raging within*, where <u>reactions and reactivations of events are front stage center in an idle mind</u>! It is as if the Ego is looking for a way to get into mischief! These episodes can last a few* *seconds to months and even years. Self-talk can even be <u>engulfing to the point of causing sleepless nights</u>, and <u>loss of good health if not controlled!</u> As an aware Self-observer and Chela, you will surely want to have a grip on this, if such symptoms as these be yours.*

> *Have you heard the expression 'the war in the mind manifests itself as a battle in the body? (Nota Bene.*

  Re-focusing your Self-talk is surely possible with *conscious, diligent patience,* redirecting your own attention to higher dimensions, positive trains of *thought, worthy projects, loved ones, attention to self-nourishing activities, career, pleasantries, communion with Spirit, meditation, and the like. Completions and resolutions are also immensely effective in re-directing Self-talk. Have you tried?*
  Remember that Balanced positive Self-talk brings rewards of inner peace that you can appreciate in your waking and sleeping moments alike.

Last and not least, a reality check on overconfidence, arrogance, or cockiness can hold your Self-talk in check, devoid of illusion which sometimes creeps in, yes?

We must give patience its due at this point.
As in all Spiritual pursuits, <u>patience</u> is paramount, and Self-talk needs patience as a full partner!

Questionable Self-talk habits are easily formed and can be difficult to break, especially those habits that have been running wild and amiss ... for years and years on end, ... during a <u>lifetime of undisciplined internal chatter</u>.

The trick here is to <u>catch yourself</u> drifting off into the old 'idle mind arena' where emotions are pulled into the negative and neutral emotional zones, *rather than playing in the positive zone. A detailed explanation is written in Chapter III of Spirit's book 'The Saint Germain Chronicles Collection',*

Gordon W. Corwin II aka Lah Rahn Ananda, Amazon. I suggest you make this a resource!

Self-ranting and Obsession is a Self-talk behavior worth noting, *even if you haven't already <u>consciously</u> experienced it personally.*

*This type of ranting is usually connected to vivid reactivations of current or past scenarios in One's life **or** past lives.*

Self-ranting can recall the fire and impassioned emotions of the original scenario (incident) and even add to its intensity when this internal mental ranting gets really hot! Notice that hanging on to old grudges can contribute to your rants. *Repetitive rantings* can become *habitual carbon copy duplicates* of former rants, making this whole disempowering and sometimes haunting self-drama and downward spiral sound like a broken record playing in your head! This could be obsession. Rantings are Self-played, and also often played and replayed to others, until listeners are no longer willing to listen to the drama! How do you break the cycle? Read on, My Dear Friends.

Rants that emanate from Upsets, can have understandable causes, some are easily identified. *You can recognize these and clear them out, in person, or in Spirit, or both.* Clearings will be discussed in more detail in the following Chapter on Emotions.

☙❧

Upsets. As pointed out by Werner Erhard, causes of upsets can be boiled down to some basics. Being fully aware of these basics need be one of your highest *relationship prioritie*s.

Throughout the Divine Realm there is an axiom, a Law, which is the *Law of Divine Order*. It is the first law of the Divine. Along your path, as your life-stream unfolds, you will find at some point that your quality of life, *if filled with peace and harmony,* **must include wisely setting your PRIORITIES.**

ON the flip side, if your priorities are out of order and out of alignment, *there will be a cost.* As you have no doubt already experienced, the cost of unwise priorities can be high and may result in you dealing with an *upset that has been thusly created.*

In brief, basic causes of Upsets can be tagged (categorized), so you can get a better grasp on the big picture when they happen to you!

- **Unmet expectation**
- **Thwarted intention**
- **Undelivered communication**

Unmet expectations. As you look to the future or deal in the present, you naturally set up expectations. If you are attached to these *expectations*, and they don't happen, then they can become painful upsets.
If you are sufficiently aware, you recognize the costs of attachment, and see it coming, *and you can separate your clear intention from attachment to an outcome.* In this context, *without attachment*, there is no suffering and no upset.
Re-read this above paragraph if you will, please.
This discipline of avoiding expectations per se is important for your understanding, and can be put into your Being with practice!

Thwarted intentions. This is another source of upset that is similarly related to *the degree of attachment to* *intentions* that One may have. *An aware Chela can recognize the emotional pattern they are having, handle the attachment (perhaps with an alternative Win-Win solution), by simply AVOIDING <u>creating some potential anger or hatred, or judgments, or rage, or revenge, etc., ... and end it with no upset.</u> Forgiveness is also part of this process, and We realize this is easier said than done; nonetheless, it is your CHOICE to face! Chapter 10 addresses forgiveness in some depth.*

Undelivered Communication. This can take two forms, as **Werner Erhard** pointed out:

1. *Something you wanted to communicate is blocked* by that person, because they are in denial or not willing to hear. Then you feel incomplete, and possibly upset.
2. *Some information is withheld from you*, for whatever reason, or it is distorted and changed to suit the delivering person's own ends and wishes. You feel manipulated, deceived, and possibly angry inside your upset.

Breaking the Cycle
Now that you have been exposed to …

- Some inner workings of Self-talk,

- Patterns of behavior inside of Self-talk,

- Sources of upsets, and

- Traps of upset habits you can fall into,

- What changes can you instill in your NEW behavior patterns to break out of these entangling cycles of relationship life?

- What can you choose to do about shifting energy you place on those breakdowns that may cling to you?

- What actions of consciousness can you bring into play, providing completion and end to more possible suffering,

- And yes, how about some *peace of mind*? Translation: *Freedom?*

Let us now speak of Changing of Self-talk.

When upset befalls you, the consciousness may see it as unwanted change, *which in itself brings potential upset to some, although not to others. You must recognize this by now?*
    If you <u>alter your reaction pattern to change</u>, holding it as a positive step in freeing yourself from the cycle, your Ego can more easily step to the side, and allow a breakaway from your own Status Quo clinging ... versus staying <u>inside the upset ... and a breakthrough into the Win-Win arena</u>.

Ego will try its best to hold you prisoner in the illusion that 'you are <u>always</u> right, especially about the ingredients of an upset, perhaps a raging fire within you'. **Now comes the choice of change aligned with reality.**

Is it also possible that there is a part of this upset that you are overlooking? Is it possible that all or part of the upset causes are out of your CONTROL, and as a Human you could choose to regard this as simply *what is*? Or possibly you are lacking further information? Questions worth meditating upon!

Where are you going to place your ENERGY? Upset or solution? Remember, the Wolf that Wins the battle is the one you feed?

Alright! So here it is. When you surrender to what is (or was), shifting your conscious energy to create a fresh approach or a Win-Win solution, and habitually <u>repeating this NEW solution in your Self-talk</u> (drowning out the old disempowering chatter), … <u>then and only then can a stubborn Ego turn loose of you to move on!</u>

In this shifting of energy, you must be totally <u>honest with yourself</u> about **your intentions and the purity of your thoughts in Self-talk.**

Otherwise, We see an Ego deceiving a fool. Both are wasting their time.

⊱⊰

Note here, if you will, some of <u>your favorite Self-talk themes</u>, maybe even mantras by now, *especially* if obsession be yours. Remember to create your self-supportive talk to be positive, optimistic, realistic and sustaining to ground your best attributes within! Be honest as you write!

We observe in some cases that certain Ones have *a higher level of Self-talk authenticity and vibration, inside and out, that would reflect and project an usual amount of concordance! In short, this means these Ones are grounded and in Divine alignment!*
Bravo to this level of authenticity, Dear Ones!

In a sense, your Self-talk defines a large part of who you really are *at the core level.*

Egos will try their best to hold you prisoner in the illusion that 'you are <u>always</u> right, especially about the grisly ingredients of an upset on fire within you.

Now come your Self-talk choices:

> Are you going to stay INSIDE the Upset or now choose to stand OUTSIDE of the Upset with a new perspective?

❦❦

Note here, if you will, some of <u>your</u> favorite **Self-talk themes**, *maybe even mantras by now*, especially if obsession be yours.

Remember the Self-supportive talk, positive and optimistic and sustaining your grounded attributes within!

_____
_____
_____
_____
_____
_____
_____
_____
_____
_____
_____
_____
_____
_____
_____
_____
_____
_____
_____
_____

"You only have the right to pursue happiness; you have to catch it yourself." — Ben Franklin

**And lastly,
Your Self-talk versus Your Outward talk.**

Be careful and conscious that the outward face you project may <u>cleverly conceal your inward agenda secrets, intentions, and ambitions</u> ... <u>secrets unrevealed and possible hyprocisy disguised by the thin veneer that would deceive.</u> Purified habits and Authenticity have their just rewards, Folks!

<u>Managing Self-talk becomes an ongoing self-discipline to which a wise and aware One will <i>devote needed attention</i></u> in the moment, ongoingly noting and adjusting the vibration it is creating .

Blessings to All,

Saint Germain

Through Lah Rahn Ananda aka Gordon Corwin II

Chapter 7

Discovering Your Triggers

The Hot Buttons

"The closer to the heart, the harder it hits!"

In this Chapter, <u>the 'I' factor comes into play</u>, asking you to address your own *triggering Hot Buttons*, those sensitive emotional spots that can flare and cause heated reaction, both positive and negative at times. Triggers can escalate into joy, happiness, euphoria, erotica, Love, compassion, and more. Likewise, Triggers may initiate disruption, aggravation, anger, envy, jealousy, grief (make your own list) to yourself and others, ... *until the triggers are identified, fully owned, and controlled through a process of Mastery over time.*

The intention of this Chapter is *to enlighten you in your process of Mastering your own Triggers!*

We have previously spoken to you about attending to the quality of your Self-talk, such that you nourish yourself with *a personal conversation of inner purity* that supports a positive attitude approach, happiness, joy, productivity, self-esteem, (and much more), ... to *then live* your moments with this harmony and inner peace you create!

Remember that *triggers of joy* **are also in the mix as elating tidbits, ... as gifts of Being Human!**

    This Chapter will discuss some of those triggered hot-button energies that could hold you back from achieving a pinnacle state of Being, particularly related to your Relationships. Hot button energies within, once recognized, are prime <u>indicators of *healings in need of your immediate* attention to process into evolved ways of Being</u>!

    Also, yet to come in this book, is the special Chapter 13 entitled 'Perspectives about Us' pointing to the power of coordinated teamwork, where self-centered Ego is put aside in favor of a bonded harmonious and healthy relationship(s) of joy in togetherness.

    Your abilities to effectively heal the triggers of Hot Buttons directly related to successful entry to The 'Us' and We of relationship. Soon you will see the interlocking magic of all the Chapters in this book, interrelating the basic and fundamental elements of relationship that all overlap,sometimes within grey areas and nonetheless, are ultimately tied together as one.

Yes indeed, your Triggers are a *biggie* (as you would say), a touchy and seemingly private, secret territory within the depths of you. Except, truth be known, others can see them more easily, from the outside looking in. So really, how secret are your 'secret' trigger buttons?

You must be absolutely honest and self-forgiving as you fully tackle this healing process and fully own it as yours. Now you will be digging deeply into the depths of yourself and *discovering your own triggers*. Yes, this can be a bit unnerving at first.

Admitting these traits is *like making a confession by yourself to yourself*. That's the first challenge.

Next is authentically exposing these triggers. Then thirdly, correcting and changing your reactive behaviors *in full view of your partner(s)!* Oh My! A big humbling assignment? I didn't promise you a rose garden, Folks, and still, roses can be yours as you mine the gold of this Mastery. This is the gold. It is yours for the taking.

As Saint Germain, I promise Mastery to the faithful, dedicated and courageous students diligently persevering to seek a higher vibrational life of aligned purpose!

Under the surface, this is all about Change and Mastery, which takes courage both at the start and in actually following through, <u>without exceptions or excuses</u>.

Only after you've Mastered these fundamental building blocks of which I speak, and their use in your life, will you see the bloom on these roses! Know as you start your process that Triggers can be very subtle and cleverly disguised by self-illusion. Later, with experience, you will catch yourself, *and only by <u>brutal self-honesty</u>. Then you are ready to mine the gold of the inner truths you are looking for!*

Many triggers originate from early childhood memories, experiences, and learned behavior from family. As you will see from the examples below, they vary infinitely from person to person.

Often when triggers happen, they are directly linked to an upset. General types of upsets are discussed in this book in the Chapters entitled EMOTIONS and SELF-TALK. However, for now, let it be simplified here.

Again, recall that basic causes of Upsets can be tagged (categorized), so you can get a better grasp on the big picture <u>when they happen to you</u>!

- Unmet expectation *
- Undelivered communication
- Thwarted intention

There is one more cause: * Unfulfilled <u>*priorities*</u>!

Various friends and colleagues of the Author have been interviewed to uncover *their* particular random set of hot button triggers, a*s visible* *examples* for you to then compile your OWN list. Depending upon the quality and completeness of *your* individual list, you will generate *infinitely valuable and introspective material to work with during this process. And remember please that as you launch this process*, you will discover **new** Triggers that need be added to your list. *(Eventually you will get the big ones tacked). Be brutally honest with yourself and thereby be eligible to get* healing results *beyond your imagination!*

Examples of Hot Button Triggers

Interviewee:

Giving or offering love to someone and having it be refused.

Not receiving immediate satisfaction when expected.

Being ignored when sincerely trying to communicate!

Being used and/or feeling used.

Being treated unkindly and without care, especially when offering *excessive kindness beyond my boundaries*.

Being disrespected as a person.

Being unduly or unfairly judged.

Someone appreciating getting what they *want*, but *not appreciating* me who gave it to them!

Taking Me for granted, taking advantage of my kindness.

Interviewee:

Crossing agreed upon boundaries!

Breaking agreements.

Lack of integrity in personal and business dealings, or both.

Misleading communications and withholding information!

Being irresponsible.

Broken promises - agreements.

Refusal to 'clear up' and discuss a misunderstanding.

Having to admit that I screwed up, *was wrong.*

Others refusals to accept my *excuses* as justifiable!

Someone's insistence on getting their 'want' when my 'need' is pressing and clearly a higher priority!

Constantly being made wrong, while the Ego person insists they are 'always right'... about everything.

Being stepped on, while another proceeds to get what they want.

Narcissistic behaviors from one *claiming to be a friend.*

Interviewee:

Being ignored.

Receiving passive aggressive behavior from another.

Broken promises.

Refusal to communicate!

Being used as an emotional release dumpster!

Denial and annoyance when asked to clear up a mess!

Untrustworthy actions!

Not being acknowledged for worthy and positive things I do!

Not being thanked and appreciated when I deserve it!

Not saying 'I'm sorry' when it is appropriate.

Insistence upon indefinitely deferring discussion on confrontational issues.

Disagreeable Emotional outbursts at me *while I'm helping them.*

Ungrateful actions and behaviors.

My needs ignored! Will not listen.

My good word being doubted – being treated with suspicion.

Interviewee:

Being betrayed!

Abandonment.

Being Ghosted!

Being forced to obey orders from uninformed and incapable people.

Violating my *'imagined' right of entitlement* to *be treated kindly.*

Needing to confront others who have anger.

Being neglected when attention is warranted.

MY well-being, uncared for, neglected, or defied.

Not getting my fair share.

Being lied to and deliberately / secretly deceived.

Disregard from Narcissistic people, about my feelings.

Being taken advantage of when I'm down and under duress.

Unmet expectations.

Getting back selfishness in return for generosity!

Ungratefulness when I AM generous and kind.

Interviewee:

Being treated UNFAIRLY!

Dealing with demanding and unknowledgeable female supervisors.

Co-workers not doing their job and leaving me extra work.

Refusal to be open and hear my feelings.

My clear needs being ignored.

  Refusing to make exceptions to the rules, for my benefit.

  Demanding people who are in positions of authority.

  Selfishness.

Others who show up for Me as ignorant.

Uneven exchange of relationship energy, when I'm on the short end.

Being Unchosen or chosen last.

Interviewee:

Inconsiderate people I deal with.

Ignoring my well-being – not caring about me.

Wasting my time!

Demanding from me vs. asking.

Dropping out of communication with me.

Ignoring our Agreements.

Untrustworthy actions.

    Trigger points or Hot buttons give you clues about how and when you may react emotionally. During Human lifetimes, emotions flood in on a regular basis, although sometimes disguised. It is part of being Human. Notice in this sampling of Interviewees, *how many of your commonalities* that show up in these lists! Mark them for yourself. Add in your own.

    Notice also your Ego tendencies to be lured into *justified alliance* with the **Interviewees** who have the same hot buttons and therefore you can believe that these are really justifiable as O.K for you too and need no attention! The joke is on you!

As you may notice, when you share some common triggers *with* *Interviewees, take heart that you are not alone in the healings that lie ahead. These may be valuable mirrors reflecting back to you images of yourself. Do you see how others share in the Human condition as well as you? With these reflections, can you now be more clear that Humans are all One? Food for thought!*

The question before you is: how are you going to treat these triggered emotions, using your powers *of free-will choice* and discipline? Are you going to move the energy into the *neutral or positive zones as soon as possible*, or leave it in the negative zone? Ah yes, Dear Friends, you will be asking yourself 'where is my patience when I need it most'?

Human Interactions

As We have put forth to you on repeated occasions in the *Saint Germain Chronicles Collection Book (Amazon, Lah Rahn Ananda/Gordon Corwin II)*, continued progress in your new career endeavors depends in a great part upon your learning to polish up your *skills of Human interactions.*

Your capabilities to effectively synchronize events between individuals, relationship partners, groups, and institutions, ... is your task at hand, such that interactions with yourself *begin to intermesh in harmony*, <u>without great effort on your part when your triggers are under control.</u>

Your relationships are meant to be pleasant, effective, emotionally balanced, and to serve your highest aligned purpose with honor. <u>You can be Master of your emotions</u> *or let your emotions be Master of you! Which are you?*

As We have said in earlier transmissions, fear and greed are the two primary emotions that react to **CHANGE.** This scenario is massive on your Earth at this juncture. However, there is a wide range of Human emotions that accompany these two primary emotions, fear and greed.

Your scale of emotions can play like musical notes in your body, and often not in harmony! Sometimes they play in sequence as I describe below, sometimes pleasing, ... and at other times they play the same old discordant tune <u>*every time that particular Trigger or Change or Fear rolls around for you.*</u>

These emotional notes can play tunes in unpredictably random orders that you have never experienced before, <u>sometimes striking dissonant chords that cause you much alarm and consternation.</u>

As you interact with relationship partners, colleagues, clients and contacts, *the professional manner and heightened <u>vibrations housed in your voice and body</u> are of gargantuan importance to your success in Relationship. Now is your chance to discern, learn, and then to shine, Dear Ones! You are born to shine!*

A*s triggers are activated, We point out that your responses after* consideration *need to address the truth of the situation and with complete* <u>honesty</u>… *so the healing can begin!* This honesty may or may not make you right! Oh My! 'What about my Ego?'

In your relationship, the unalterable standards of supreme ethics ask to speak out, and need to *be forever practiced and delivered without exception.* <u>Such ingrained and automatic behavior</u> *(both inward thoughts and outward behaviors) shall hold you in the finest regard with colleagues and with Our recognition for preservation of your* <u>Sacred Divine Partnership with the Holy Spirit.</u>

With experience in this process *you can learn to make these ethical choices as replies (rather than defensive or offensive as reactions), with* **<u>automaticity and in real time</u>, believe it or not.**

Trust that We are now seeing this happening with dedicated students of conscious evolution!

An accurate knowledge of your trigger points is a real gift and a leg-up in your process of relating in harmony with ease and grace. *Is this not what you have dreamed of in relationship? Also, remember that when triggered, it can be a wise idea to ask for more information, on the spot, not later, before giving your <u>reply,</u> in lieu of that knee jerk <u>reaction</u> that is likely without the training that We seek to deliver to you! We say often to 'ask for more information',* as this often can clear up the energies gone askew, and lead the way to proposing a **Win-Win solution** *to the issue, avoiding possible unnecessary emotional confrontations.*

Remember, you're only going to be as good at this healing process as you want to be. We can guide you and be with you in your process, and yet we are not promising to do it for you. This is your relationship training and your lifetime!

> 𝓗ealing the effect of your own '𝓣riggers' is meant for people that are brave enough to heal their own '𝓔motions'.

As you perfect managing your Hot Buttons and their effect upon your behaviors, *be aware that <u>YOU are the one in control</u>, <u>bringing positive,</u>*

loving, Win-Win solutions to the table through leadership, *regardless of your position on the ranking scale! (When your own triggers are well-managed and transmuted, you avoid being the one that brings naked problems to the relationship table. Your role is now transformed!*

You become part of the solution and not the problem.

MY TRIGGER POINTS   Date:

_____
_____
_____
_____
_____
_____
_____
_____
_____
_____
_____
_____
_____
_____
_____
_____
_____
_____
_____
_____

_____
_____
_____

Have you been Honest with yourself?

Now here comes the real payoff. As your triggering incidents show up and flare up, and likely have their way with you, **this is the time to formally write down the life's lesson(s) that this situation is showing you!** We emphasize this, as it is the payoff that is so often overlooked. The *typical behavior* is to find a coping solution, just get there somehow, and to use a convenient *Bandage for the moment*. Erase the *'give me hope, help me cope'* approach! Aligned Action is the worthy companion of Hope!

Guess what, Folks? Its guaranteed that *dangling life's lessons* will keep showing up in your life, repeating over and over and over again until Mastered. Karma plays a mysterious hand in the game of consciousness evolution. Is the Universe telling you something?

For your growth and Well-being, We pray that you will use the space below to begin conscientiously noting several pertinent points **about each life's lesson (not the dramas) you are handed. Be strict with yourself, summarize and hit your target!**

**THE TRIGGER + THE Incident in BRIEF
+ THE LIFE'S LESSON   Date**

_____
_____
_____
_____
_____
_____
_____
_____
_____
_____
_____
_____

In the months to follow, do yourself a favor and review and update the worksheets in this Chapter, and <u>note your progress.</u> Report back to Me monthly if you are wise.

We celebrate your victories with you, as you put each new notch in your belt of higher vibrational accomplishments along the path of your Spiritual journey.

In time, why not become a Connoisseur of Personal Relationships that Sing to your Soul!
It is worth the effort!

Be well and be obedient to the Laws of the Universe providing access to these gifts of Light, joy, and purification of  your consciousness. Those dedicated to rising up into the ExtraOrdinary, encased in a Capsule of Divine Wisdom, ... shall be given gifts of grace and showered with synchronicities of life that are beyond your dreams.
Know that your courage is deeply and infinitely appreciated and acknowledged from Above, My Dearest Ones.

Many Blessings in the Light,

Saint Germain and the Realm

Through Lan Rahn Ananda aka Gordon Corwin II 10-25-19

Chapter 8

Emotions

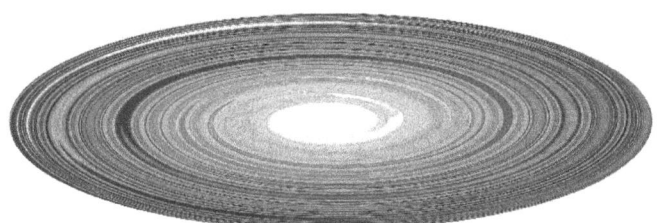

Inner Thoughts and Feelings

Mastering Human emotions is clearly at or near the top of the stack of challenges for aspiring relationship partners. Emotions can be viewed as various states of consciousness that flow through the mind and body in response or reaction to certain stimuli including change from the Status Quo, often used as a comfort zone haven.

About Emotions in words of the Author, *"Over the years, I have observed that Emotions, in a sense, are handed to us by ourselves. They seem to reflect the influence of our deeply imbedded belief systems holding life experiences, learned behavior and tradition, opinions, Soul memories, facts of Truth, illusions, and the whole gamut. While overwhelming at times, I Am truly grateful for our Human abilities to individually experience the inflow, and at the same time to have the free-will choice about how we handle and process these thoughts and feelings that Lord Saint Germain calls emotions". Lah Rahn*

Saint Germain resumes,

These states can encompass love, fear, joy, hate, sorrow, anger, elation, bliss ... you can add in your own. Observe for yourselves, as you will be later asked to so do in this Chapter!

In Spirit, We place great importance on your learning to deal *successfully* with your wild fluctuation of emotions, thus opening your Beloved gateway into new, more peaceful, and harmonious states of a higher vibrational consciousness.

In contrast, by ignoring emotional awareness and training, you will likely have a bumpy road in relationship pursuits, often having to move on and start new ones, over and over again, *only to have your same initiations repeated.* Have you heard of Karma?

Emotions go hand in hand *with strong feelings ... intuitions that are taking place within you, often in habitual or involuntary responses to stimuli.*

> *We support converting emotional reactions into constructive vibrations, after consideration, using patience, gaining needed missing information, and using your power to create Win~Win solutions.*

Throughout the recorded history of your World, Mankind has struggled, without great success, about learning to effectively manage at a conscious level its inborn stream of Human emotions, while life-streams are being constantly flooded with changing energies.

Be aware that Emotions forever reappear as an integral God-given ingredient of *the Human Condition*, **embedded in your inheritance as you incarnate into each new life**.

Your opportunity for Mastery of the Human Condition is at the forefront where these emotions play a leading role.

In Earth times of massive social Change, Human emotions will predictably run rampant. Of these, fear is the most pronounced, coupled with greed.

Fear of Change among Mankind is one of the oldest emotional challenges that plague. This particular challenge plagues Humans incessantly, being motivated, strangely enough, by instincts to survive. Fear of change can equally crop up with Spirit seekers *in the pursuit of higher consciousness into the White Light ... appearing as strange and new to them.*

About Change, Accomplishment, and Sacrifice

He who would accomplish little must sacrifice little;
He who would achieve much must sacrifice much;
He who would attain highly must sacrifice greatly.
                              Quotation from James Allan

As Lord El Morya has spoken, 'The next step is to Master your positive use of the emotions that flood your minds, bellies and entire bodies. These energies that seemingly invade your consciousness can truly be managed such that *your full range of emotions is welcomed in by your own belief system, as they instantly crop up in real time, ... as you say'.*

Once Mastered, *these incoming emotions offer no further threat or concern,* as their life's reactions are wisely and simply managed and balanced *with effortless automaticity, transcending far beyond illusions that you may now believe are true, ... prior to Mastery training.*

***This* Gateway path of emotional Mastery can lead *you* to such evolvement, with results that will harmonize your life in ways you cannot now imagine!** If you are willing, as We proceed with you who engage over your next 3 months, notice *your* progress in this regard as you *willingly choose* to put Our teachings into practice (momentarily, daily, and on-goingly).

During this process, *You will attract more Light and notice it! Others may notice it in you also, ... <u>without your prompting</u>, as you are a humble Being seeking evolvement and desiring not to self-aggrandize.*

Once Mastered, your fluctuating range of emotions can *actually serve you well,* believe it or not, adding spice and variety to your life, in addition to the opportunities for growth in managing them! Ease and Grace follows Mastery, Dear Friends. <u>Yes, I AM speaking</u> about this *tangible quality of your daily Earth-life!*

As Lord Saint Germain, (to continue) *I speak of emotions with respect to relationships, peace of mind, manifested results, harmony, self-confidence, and countless other parts of your life. Some core level training is required, however.*

Can you imagine how <u>just a few of your challenging emotions</u> *could handily be transformed to serve you well? What would these be? Example emotions could include: Love, euphoria, deep satisfaction, peacefulness, serenity, inspiration, enthusiasm, indifference, frustration, disillusionment, anger, hate, rage, and so on. Write some of your current emotions on paper, here and now, before we proceed.*

My Challenging Emotions

_____
_____
_____
_____
_____
_____

_____
_____
_____
_____
_____

❦

Recognizing Emotions in the moment

*N*ow *We speak about <u>coupling</u> clear recognition and identification of incoming/ongoing emotions with choice and action.* Our teachings combine this Self-observing discipline with *your conscious action to manage emotions.*

Recognizing and feeling your emotions as they flow in is the first step toward managing the effects and then ultimately becoming FREE from being held slave to an unruly part of yourself!

Application of this combination ...of *discipline with conscious action ... will lead you into an unbelievable new space, peace, joy, and Blessings of Grace beyond your current beliefs.*

This is a *promise* from Above, **if you follow My directions.** And yes, there are conditions, as you might expect by now. Please take note that some of my well-known compulsory *corollaries are attached to My promises for your success.* So read on, Good People. Many Monkeys will be lifted from your backs, ... those burdens you have carried for years with no end in sight.

୧୬‍ଏ

Managing Your Emotions with *Care*

All Humanity is Blessed with the birthright to receive emotions. They can be regarded as pleasurable, loving and heartfelt, and also challenging, negative, painful, and burdensome, if that be your choice. Regardless, this flood of energy is an internal visceral force that needs to be actively reckoned with, ... managed with care especially by all aspiring Spirit seekers and Chelas, and others as they step up.

We applaud you for your awareness and responsibility of conduct, as aware Ones seeking Light, to raise your vibration, personally and in relationship concert with others.

On your Earth plane you have no doubt noticed that a certain large number of your Earth populous has chosen to let their emotions run rampant, ... *without management or care or regard about the effects and consequences their unmanaged 'run wild' emotions can have upon fellow Humans and upon the* *collective as well.* Just observe the careless, rampant use of inflammatory emotional outbursts by your cadre of 'politicians' claiming to be leaders!

Now, We offer some guidance about <u>responsibly</u> handling, caring for, and constructively using emotions as they flood your Being, inflowing on a momentary basis.

Remember, We Ascended, have personal experience in this department, as We were once fully incarnated … with emotions in hand. Now Ascended as We are, emotions have been replaced by the Truth of Oneness which binds Us together. This has occurred after many lifetimes on the Karmic wheel, prior to our Ascensions, to now serve Humanity from Above.

Here is the point. Some of you on Earth at this time are continuously tempted to 'air' your <u>*raw emotions*</u> with great vigor, releasing them by speaking, electronic communications, writings, body language, etc.

Ideally, conscious Ones will first be aware of an emotion in the moment. They will consider it, consciously internalizing the energy, making a choice of its highest and best use, and <u>THEN release the energy, if useful</u>. Conscious Ones will often <u>refine their raw emotion</u> **before taking action of any sort.**

Utilizing this healing process, you can Bless yourself with the *ability and habitual behavior* of 'airing' <u>*only* an emotion that you truthfully believe is merit worthy</u>! This will take observation on your part, perhaps refining a raw emotion, and removing Ego with discipline from indulgence.

Do you know that some emotions you receive and hold as yours are <u>meant for you personally</u>, *as information or lessons from Spirit, and <u>not necessarily in need of sharing or airing?</u>*

<u>On the obverse side of that coin</u> are those masses of you that irresponsibly and blatantly blurt out emotions as they are received, popping off with Ego run wild, speaking off, ranting, raving, in full defiance of any possible effect upon their audience! Such behavior ignores any consideration of merit worthiness as such oblivious behavior surrounds shared emotion(s). Some such behaviors can have Karmic implications! **This is especially true for those Ones of you who know better!**

**A favorite excuse is:
'I'm just saying what I feel'!
What they (you) feel does not necessarily merit being shared ... or contribute to your audience ... it may actually injure them! Have you ever considered this?**

So, what is the payoff for the irresponsible 'pop-off ranter' before using any care and management of their stream of emotions? The payoff for these loose cannons in their selfish actions, is an Ego satisfaction that of reckless and self-centered indulgence in an emotional release, often of turmoil, frustration, anger or chaos. These Egos have given full permission to their <u>unenlightened hosts</u> to <u>ignore the consequences of irresponsible behavior that may follow, allowing them to dominate, manipulate, and always be right!</u> Such behavior of your **'pop-off ranters' moves them several rungs downward on the Spiritual Ladder.** Does this ring a bell for you?

We see a blinding contrast of Beings here ... some aware and seeking alignment or the obverse Ego ranter. Managed emotions or wild emotional behavior is a startling contrast, revealing gigantically opposing degrees of awareness and core consciousness!

For those Ones of you being <u>responsible for managing and caring for your emotions</u>, We applaud you once again as you are seeking increased beams of Light to raise your vibration, personally *and* in concert with others.

<u>Your motivation to also handle emotions with love and care is commendable and observable from Above by Ourselves in the greatest of love and gratitude.</u>

Your *presence* among fellow Humans is also a gift to Humanity when emotions are managed as some of you so aptly <u>demonstrate.</u> Continued discipline of the ***<u>Emotions Management process</u>*** will take you to great heights, as you Ascend the rungs of the Spiritual ladder. Know that you are Loved and acknowledged. **Blessings to you.**

Here now **We bring particular attention to the commonly seen emotion of <u>anger</u>.**

As mentioned elsewhere in this work, We leave secular 'anger management therapy' to your professionals to guide you and assist in converting anger emotions, if needed, into the positive zone that can then serve you. Also, you have within your reach My new book: '**The Saint Germain Chronicles Collection**', **Lah Rahn Ananda aka Gordon Corwin II, Amazon,** *which gives unparalleled attention to management of emotions and related healings throughout various Chapters.*

Insights at this point are meant to be included for your healing, enlightenment, Mastery and ultimately for your Freedom!

**Anger is an Ego indulgence that Humans can choose to 'fall into' when other alternatives are not seen or chosen
in the heat of the moment.**

Lapsing into this emotional state of anger is actually one's Self-choice, to dive into various captive semi-paralyzed states of mind, where capabilities are BLINDED and BLOCKED in favor of indulging in an Ego-filled lower vibration, believed to be satisfying in some fashion. *Freedom now becomes sacrificed and is lost in these moments.*

Emotional <u>release</u> techniques can be learned and then done in private, often times a lengthy drama with

---

**The One who becomes angry
has become
a captive of their own device!**

Another person hearing your small story for the 'umpteenth time', as you say, until the energy disburses. <u>After</u>

emotional release, Ones are more grounded to then process raw emotions into refined choices of response, as I have mentioned. Sound familiar?

However, here We want for you to get to *the root of the anger mechanism within you.*

Notice in your own experiences, when white hot anger has taken you over, ... how crippled, fractured and compromised becomes *your ability to use your otherwise rational choices to deal with an emotional situation.* This state is sometimes called 'seeing red'.

*** With your full capabilities in place, however, an issue can be recognized as needing immediate constructive attention, and using your power of OBSERVATION, **replacing** the anger reaction, so the next step of resolution can proceed in motion.

*** Here you have *skipped and bypassed the Anger step* altogether, just as you are learning to *observe and then skip the judgment step* on the way to filing an objective experience of 'what is' into your belief system. Can you see how this relieves you of being burdened and shouldering and cementing in place an opinion that may or may not hold any truth! ***

> *Moreover, for Advanced Spiritual Beings on the Earth-plane, indulgence in anger-filled reactions is now an Ego luxury that you can ill afford.* Nota Bene! Saint Germain.

In place of this Ego satisfying choice of anger, We suggest an immediate <u>healing pause</u> allowing you to:

    Take a deep breath,

    Bring in Patience,

    Find out what information may be missing,

    Consider new perspective(s),

    Forgive from your emotional heart level,

    And then calmly reply (or not react), and *after consideration, accessing/creating a Win-Win solution.*

Practice these steps, in sequence, and you will see the difference in outcomes. Feel the levity and let the Light Shine In! *Your best replaces your worst?*

Consider a common sequence in an *Anger scenario*:

You have habitual patterns of behavior, yes?
You have habitual upset *default response patterns*, yes?
Now an upset surfaces, let's say you regard it as serious.   Emotion strikes.

The anger upset scenario may be escalated from:

- Annoyance   to
- Frustration   to
- Impatience   to
  <u>**To your choice of a default reaction**</u>*:*
  Anger? Or Flight?

(Here is the fork in the road, Folks. Another choice)

A Choice to PAUSE, OBSERVE WHAT IS, REFINE,   FORGIVE, and CREATE WIN-WIN SOLUTIONS.

Uncovering <u>missing information</u>, and using this constructive behavior are keys to creating a Win-Win solution.

You are aware, of course, that solutions can be Win-Win, win-lose, lose-win or lose-lose? Give this some thought as We proceed together?

In Short, just Skip the Anger choice, *if that be your current stress - default action,* and defer to this choice of constructive behavior as your <u>new default response pattern</u>. As you practice this new habit pattern, be patient with yourself **and** with this process, *enjoying the ease and grace you receive!*

Congratulations! You are now making your new default pattern an automatic part of your behavior, especially when you hit the speed bumps.

৵৶

Do you recall from prior words in this Chapter, Our training about 'avoiding Judgments'? Remember how you were trained to skip the *Judgment choice*, and let the Observation move straight away into your belief system as simply *'what is'?*

*** Now. here again, is your <u>parallel healing training</u> about 'Avoiding Anger'... Strikingly parallel if you can relate the two processes.

Anger is an emotional reaction of choice at some level. <u>The heart of this enlightened anger process is to completely skip the Anger choice</u> altogether as an unneeded step in handling an upset, and to move directly into observation (an aware choice), as in constructive behavior, and then to FORGIVENESS, if relevant, *into open space for arriving at a Win-Win solution!* ***

❦

Very importantly, to now clarify Our intention about the true meaning of Win-Win solutions … contrasted to a mere compromise, please make this distinction:

Know that a mere compromise brings elements to the table which commonly satisfy some of the needs/wants/requests of each partner, BUT it leaves out, by definition, other parts wanted/needed/requested by the other party(s). So where does that leave the relationship partners about being supported and satisfied about their next attitudes and moves *in an effort to continue in harmony?*

"The compromise, as a well worn out solution, is so well known in your World, deeply impregnated with a Third Dimensional Consciousness that buys the Human Illusion as its flawed truth".

Being left dissatisfied or in emotional limbo *casts its own shadow on the (sometimes coping) compromise just reached, even though agreed upon.*

Agreement**,** (not necessarily full-hearted), surrender, acceptance, good faith and detachment *can* hold a compromise in place in the moment … and then again, *will it be lasting? We would sponsor the Divinely- sourced solution that transcends compromise! Read on, Dear Ones.*

It should come as no surprise by now that climbing the rungs of the Spiritual ladder does, in fact, involve application of life-long energy of dedication, change and perseverance on the part of the aspiring Chela, Light Carrier, and student of life.

We note from Above that, currently, the vast majorities of Human choices are made on a <u>*reactive basis*</u>, *ignoring* <u>the powerful potential of choosing to wisely manage emotions on a **conscious basis at the time the emotion presents**</u>!

Reactions of Status Quo choice seem to be the behaviors of most. *Remember, defaulting to the Status Quo is <u>actually a choice</u>*!

> *Here now, We have shown you the way out of this dangerous reactive behavior trap and pattern often entangling you in negative results, showing up every Earth-day upon your International stage and upon your own personal stage where you are the actor, front and center.*

☙❧

A quiet Mind. You must accept and trust the fact that entering this Gateway of emotional Mastery and *sustaining your position demands the presence of a quiet mind.* Daily Transcendental Meditation is a favored modality.

Buddha

Speaks about a Gateway
to Ascended Consciousness

'A Transcended Meditative State'

To all of My Beloved Devotees

and Truth Seekers, … A Touch Of Enlightenment.

As Buddha, I briefly join you now about a magnificent step or possible leap for you to take in your *Journey Into Practical Spirituality*. This wondrous and surely achievable state of consciousness, ... *beyond thought* ... places the Meditator *in a relaxed and peaceful space of suspended emptiness.*
You may delightfully regard this process as a true healing.

ॐ

Now that you are in tune with the Blessings of a quiet mind, let Us proceed to focus upon patterns that repeat and need attention:

Here now, you are guided to list for yourself your <u>emotions that repeat</u>, those <u>patterns</u> that deserve to be recognized and brought to aware consciousness!
These anger patterns, for example, escalating from the emotion, to frustration, to impatience, to anger, ...

emanate commonly from changes or from upsets, often as unmet expectations. **Notice there may be correlation** *between these repeating patterns and some of your Triggers and Hot Buttons that YOU have seen listed in an earlier Chapter as well.*

For those emotion(s) triggered by Upsets, note for yourself exactly <u>what that emotional trigger is,</u> so next time you will be forewarned and can identify it clearly.

_____
_____
_____
_____
_____
_____
_____
_____
_____
_____
_____
_____
_____
_____
_____
_____
_____
_____
_____
_____
_____

❧❧

Can you see how your emotions can be tied into the other fundamentals and relationship building blocks you have in your hands with this book?

We have spoken earlier of Self-talk and Self-love. As emotions grip your attention during these correction and growth periods, remember the power in your Self-talk and Self-love by choosing to see the glass as half-full versus half-empty.

*Look for the Light
and you will be surprised
when you behold its brilliance!*

Sorting this *out, as you surrender <u>to yourself</u>, may bring Light into your self-awareness and perspectives, and precipitate ahhh haaaa moments, We pray.*

Here is a Decree that merits memorization, for your instant access in times of transcending from negative vibrations into the positive zones of emotion.

DECREE

I AM joyfully willing to love, care for, and accept *each* new moment of my life as it unfolds.

Further explanation by Lord Saint Germain:

In this altered state, and in this presence, you are aligned with the vibration of creation, … you are opened to receive from the higher Dimensions. Here you are joyfully equipped to unfold your own Divine adventure in concert with your Choices.

Honor this highly coveted Earthly legacy with all the strength you can muster from your Earth consciousness and your Highest-Self, illuminated by the fire of your internal sun, the Holy Spirit. This is your *Divine Partnership*.

In conclusion, We encourage you to note your progress, with dates and results, as your considered replies replace knee-jerk reactions of habit.

You may be surprised, if not thrilled, at how this
will boil down to *a few enlightened basics* for you to
consciously apply and repeat in several different
aspects of your life,
providing joyful gifts of Mastery in Relationship!

Blessings Along Your Journey

Saint Germain and El Morya together as One

Though Lah Rahn Ananda aka Gordon Corwin II

Chapter 9

Change

"When you are finished changing, you're finished."
— Benjamin Franklin

Y**our choice, as you would have it!** *Change can be viewed from a number of different perspectives, as your consciousness and Ego will allow.*

Freely Allowing Change, *as it pops up in your life, is an attribute of consciousness of a person committed and empowered to pursue an examined Human Lifetime, leading to the ExtraOrdinary!*

And conversely, resistance to flowing with inevitable change, clinging to the Status Quo, brings with it a myriad of consequences, … which, I must add here, are deferred for another of My dissertations, My Dear Friends.

Also, We mention another impact of Change, where *you choose to initiate* and bring about new situations in your own life. Think of some examples?

_____
_____
_____
_____
_____
_____
_____
_____
_____
_____

O**pen eyes, ears and all of your senses will tell you that** *Change is commonly surrounding you upon all sides, like it or not, your choice is to flow along or resist.* No doubt you are experiencing and deeply feeling this 'change' energy in a now chaotic Earth-World, where structures are being questioned, challenged and in process of being dismantled.

Yes, change shall continue to occur as you are *no doubt experiencing and deeply feeling. Your World economies are rapidly shifting, masses of population are desperately seeking to survive as changing vulnerability rises around the Earth Globe.*

In your best interest of balance and staying grounded, your meditation practice is highly recommended at this time and must continue to accommodate the challenge of change! You are urged to set and reserve a regular clock-time each morning, and meditate <u>before any work is commenced</u>.

This will help to <u>focus and ground</u> you early on, for at least a refreshing breather in the beginning of the day. Meditating in the evening before your evening meal is a second window in the Ayurvedic vata body cycle that will also pay great dividends to <u>sustain</u> your needed energy levels in these times. Inclusion in Regular daily routines is healthy and recommended for Earth inhabitants, <u>young and old</u>.

OUTSIDE OF YOUR COMFORT ZONE

By this point, if you are authentically engaged With Us here, you will no doubt feel a squirrely restlessness taking hold, when Change is being revealed as your middle name, as it were.

Be advised that this *state of vulnerability is a location of your golden treasure* ... the growth in consciousness you and your Higher-self are seeking.

> In short, We ask that you travel here with Us to a destination of honesty and Self-commitment where YOU are restfully alert yet willing to be far *outside of your comfort zone!*

TRUST IN SPIRIT WHEN WE SAY THIS EVOLVED SPACE IS A PREFERRED ZONE FOR GROWTH AND POTENTIAL REWARDS.

At this point, <u>Your</u> *daily discipline will be required to optimize your further coaching on your Dharmic path, where some Ones of you shall begin to commune with Ourselves in greater depth.* Others who go it alone, choosing to stay stuck in their <u>Ego's illusion</u> that brings a <u>meager payoff</u> for maintaining the status quo of their morass-filled consciousness, will anchor themselves in the lower part of the The 3rd Dimension as a permanent resident! Nonetheless, Our loving offer of Blessings, Grace and Spiritual evolution in this lifetime is always open to *those who choose to re-choose, and to evolve into the attainable higher dimensions of consciousness within Human grasp.*

Alright, but 'what about Me and My relationship(s), you ask?

Change is indeed an Earthly reality of being Human, and that distresses even the best of you. And yet, those of you who have become flexible in surrendering to inevitable CHANGE, *as a routine behavior*, are to be complimented! I describe here a vital part of the *Grand Process of Consciousness Evolution*, discussed at great length in my latest book <u>The Saint Germain Chronicles Collection, 2017 Gordon Corwin II aka Lah Rahn Ananda, Amazon.</u> *If you are able to **Master** its contents, you will surely be well on your way to Enlightenment, Dear Ones!*

As a note: Change is massively ubiquitous and far reaching upon your planet, in that *it affects the plant, animal and elemental kingdoms as well as Human kind. You are not alone. Your astrophysicists will also confirm that change throughout this Universe is indeed an on-going phenomenon, and a truly amazing dynamic, witnessing the hand of God that reaches far and* wide into other Universes, through time warps, and into black holes.

In previous Chapters of this book, We have spoken about Sources of Upset *with respect to change.* Here I shall elaborate.

In the context of Change, as I speak of now, notice your newly discovered default behavior pattern(s) when the face of change is staring at you! Your self-observations will serve as guidelines for some possible self-correction, if resistance be your default behavior *where change itself* is regarded as upset. Your USA Government is now struggling to break free of the Status Quo in many of its structures and policies ... and this emphasis on change is causing unparalleled upsets in many sectors of Humanity, as you may have noticed?

How you regard change itself becomes so very important in how it affects you when it strikes. Listen to your self-talk for clues to make self-adjustments that would ease the impact of change along your journey.

On the brighter side, *often times change can be welcomed by some as a refreshing manifestation of the new, beyond the STATUS QUO!*

So it follows then, that to become a Friend of Changes is to freely make (or have made) modifications to your habit patterns, thinking, actions, and your other aligned behaviors in support of your evolution and Spiritual growth. It is good to take note that *resistance to inevitable change can pull you out of the natural flow with the synchronicity of energies on* *the move, lowering your vibratory rate from your natural God given state of abundance, happiness, peace and joy.* Were you aware of this?

Resistance to such change can be a signal to you, an opportunity for growth. If you are self-observant, you can be nicely present in these triggering moments, and tack the emotion(s) that need to be elevated into the higher zone of positive vibration!

If you are attached to something or someone, for example, and bucking the *natural order of change,* struggling as you swim upstream against the current, *note the default behaviors and self-talk that you are having.* You may be surprised about what you find lurking in the depths of your entrenched belief system, if you dare to look!

*A**lright! We must address Stuckness at this point. Stuckness** is a pattern that sometimes adheres to a student of life, a Chela, or to a simple life-*stream plodder, <u>unaware</u> of a particular behavior, until change surfaces in life's circumstances.

Once recognized and when awareness is raised about the stuckness, this <u>pattern can be broken</u> and healed, applying aligned proactive behaviors, yielding a higher and lasting vibrational energy allowing forward movement. As spoken earlier, *absolute self-honesty and discipline, devoid of excuses, must prevail here in order for <u>needed introspection</u> to have its healing way with you.*

When liberated from a stuckness in arenas of your life, We pray this *new vibration and awareness* will then adhere to you with Cosmic Glue, never to part.

We in the Realm applaud you all <u>as you relentlessly dance your way through this Human lifetime of constant change</u> and challenge and ultimately surrender unto your highest Soul-self consciousness. This is a partial ingredient of the grand *Soul merge process* I have been known to speak about.

Change can be empowering once your Ego lets go of status quo attachments, allowing you to embrace new possibilities that Spirit may be bringing your way. We give signs and information to many, and most go unnoticed. Let yourself be a sterling exception!

When massive Change confronts you personally or collectively, stirred emotion plays a massive role in the outcome.

Master your emotions, and you can become a Blessed Spiritual <u>observer</u> of your current world events, beyond the reach of troublesome anxieties.

Personally then You can become a part of the 'change solution' in alignment with Spirit and thereby cease perpetuating those unaligned outcomes which plague you.

Openness via change to fresh approaches and perspectives can support you greatly, especially <u>when you are facing initiations of detachment</u>! Inspiring energies are abundant, <u>if only you can learn to access them</u>, always available from the Universal Mind!

Becoming Part of the Change Solution

Alright, having internalized this essence of change, you are now more highly equipped to tackle these challenges which We will next bring to your attention via Chapters that follow, especially those on ATTACHMENT and DETACHMENT and MOVING ON.

Also on your plate is the Mastering of openness to receive and accept the rewards of change. Many of you are such heartful givers and this focus on always giving often blocks you *from an awareness of when and how to receive!!*

Vibrational Adjustments and Freedom

Awake, Light-bearing Humans willingly adjust to Change as it arrives. The *restfully alert* will blend these energies into their Human lives with Ease and Grace. As for lower ... you will vibrational Ones, struggle, kick, continue to a captive of shout and scream, resistance. We your own soon enough pray you will from Above to allow the Light shine in!

> *Remember, receiving is also part of the Grand Process, and you are Divinely entitled to receive with gratitude and Love.*

Freedom and Change. An unwavering faith in God's grace and Spirit's loving hands to guide you brings in a tremendous sense of Freedom, along with a knowing that the future of Earth and the Universe will unfold as it shall in accordance with Divine Law.

As Saint Germain, I encourage you to concentrate on My guidance here and mine the gold at hand. Live your conscious life each day in the Sphere of TRUTH, enjoy each moment as it presents itself, and be fully responsible for yourself, your joy, your health, your Well-being, and continue to contribute with Love and abundance to the Well-being of others in your Human sphere. As you persevere, know that you are Loved!

Many Blessings to you, brave Ones.

Saint Germain

Through Lah Rahn Ananda aka Gordon Corwin II

AFFIRMATION FOR YOUR HARVEST

"I AM joyfully *willing* to love, care for,
and accept each new
moment of My life as it unfolds. I
acknowledge *what is.*

I embrace the swinging door of *choice* to
transcend *My* old
and burdensome *judgments.*

My *life's purpose* is integrated with a clear
vision of *"Change"*
as inevitable, ... empowering Me with the
Freedom to lead an
*extraordinary examined life that is worth
living."*

Lah Rahn / Gordon Corwin 10-2013

Chapter 10

Forgiveness and Compassion

The practices of Forgiveness and Compassion are so powerful that they can lead you with ease and grace from separation into the domain of higher Love vibrations of the Universe ... a Sacred place where all need to gather for hearts to meet and Be together as One.

To begin, ... We Beings now Ascended or you now incarnated, or spinning somewhere in betwixt on the Karmic wheel, ...
were conceived of pure Love by your Creator.

And then came the creation of Human *free-will choice*, coupled with Earthly Duality. This capability and condition with its responsibilities and consequences, was given to Mankind on Earth in the beginning. These are very uniquely different powers than those vested in other Beings in other parts of this Universe.

To balance the varied uses of this free-will-choice gift, was born a myriad of consequences across the Earth, manifesting according to the wisdom <u>or</u> foolish behaviors of the choosers.

You well know that the results of free-will choice continue to be a mind-boggling mixture of magnificently aligned outcomes and also a discordant chaos of the lower vibrations. (Just take a look at your World today! Read your history books, recording over 3000 Earth years of free-will consequences, where choosers *host Ego* in favor of Spirit! The track record of Human evolution clearly speaks for itself!)

S**o, during Human incarnations,** We Ascended in Spirit hold the hearts and hands of Humans striving to reconcile problematic outcomes of circumstance and choice, offering you a means to realign with each other.

The objective of reconnecting you and your relationship partners with a higher ultimate vibration is in the spotlight as I speak, as free-will has its way with all of you!

The offering here is the Blessing of Forgiveness, Divinely hosted by Spirit through My cadre of loving and purified Ascended Masters! As Saint Germain, I AM honored to be Maha Chohan of this Domain for the next 2000 Aquarian Age Earth years.

Though Soul plans are Divinely authored in concert with many variables, Heavenly and Earthly, (that is a subject for another fine time, Folks), incarnated Earthly Beings encounter challenging lifetime circumstances *that need be ultimately resolved with each other.*

Bringing unsettled energies <u>to rest</u> **using the higher vibration of Forgiveness can magically replace discord and separation.**

You urgently need this Blessing of Forgiveness in your Spiritual toolbox! Beyond the interplay of Human free-will choice, the Human Ego in action, and inputs from a Higher-self, … <u>lies the pressing need to harmonize, blend, and synchronize otherwise discordant events,</u> as part of Mastering your life lessons offered to you this time around! *The power of Forgiveness allows you to realign into Love and Divine order what may have gone amiss somewhere in a relationship process, and now needs to be transmuted.*

Along with Forgiveness comes space for Compassion. We often note from Above that outcroppings of Compassion begin to flow freely once *Forgiveness and Acceptance of 'what is'* takes its rightful place in a consciousness.

With awareness in action, Compassion will live in you as a default habit pattern, to be deeply felt and shared when circumstances merit this Blessing.

> **Kindly remember that Compassion is linked with Forgiveness, as together they synthesize and deliver heartful energies, serving together as inseparable Partners of Love.**

Differing opinions, varied belief systems, cultures, and more can cause clashes that resist. These can remain so, <u>or</u> can *be dissolved and reconciled at the conscious heart level as Ego would allow. Are you open to Compassion?*

As a test of <u>truly forgiving from the heart</u>, or of simply just overlooking a *'burr that still grinds along under the saddle blanket'*, ask yourself if you are Forgiving or REACTIVATING the problem over again in your self-talk or conversations with others? Or has the memory been transmuted into a vibration of Love through Forgiveness, and the 'burr' no longer exists?

You have to answer this for yourself each time such incidents surface for you. **If the irritating (or worse) the Reactivation still keeps popping up,** you know that, in your heart, **you have not truly Forgiven yet.** In this case, you are wise to repeat your Forgiveness process until the slate is wiped clean!

Here is a check list that will assist in moving forward with your Forgiveness Process:

- Acknowledging any *responsibility YOU bear* in the issue at hand,
- Internalizing your acceptance that the issue really exists, versus denial or illusion to the contrary,
- Moving beyond your denial,
- Being compassionate for other person(s) feelings and triggers,
- Giving the issue any serious attention it deserves,
- Avoiding sluffing it off, *sweeping under the carpet*,
- *Speaking your forgiveness* to others, in person,
- Visualizing standing *in their shoes* looking back at yourself.
- Demonstrating Compassion in action and thought,
- Demonstrating Love
- Getting over it *yourself!*   *Forgiving yourself!*
- *Eliminate drama,*
- Grasping a *new perspective,*
- Seeking Truth over opinion and conjecture,
- Resisting temptation to over-minimize an important issue,
- Creating *new horizons of possibility to fill any gaps,*
- *Moving On with empowerment in a relationship!*

After you have diligently done your part, *whatever your process may be,* **your heart will tell you if and whether you have truly FORGIVEN.**

Then, you will feel your burden lifted by this unique gift of Forgiveness to yourself and others!
A new sense of FREEDOM that **Forgiveness provides is now YOURS!**

During the course of this lifetime, your wise and loving choice to make Forgiveness and Compassion regular practices from the core of your heart and the center of your Being will create a pathway found in no other place.

In Love and Light,

Saint Germain

With Lah Rahn Ananda aka Gordon Corwin II

Chapter 11

COMMUNICATION

"Half-wits talk much, but say little."
— *Benjamin Franklin*

> Along with vibrational interchanges, verbal and written and visual communications can, with proper care, be laced with energies to bind the very foundations creatively holding a relationship together.
>
> These quality interchanges can happen at every opportunity, using your loving will, in your conversations, letters, emails, messages, texts, notes, scribblings *and* body language, ... and much more!
>
> Speaking from the heart, authentic relationship communications carry *an even exchange of energy, positive and with love.*

Beautifully expressed in Spanish, *Un incluso intercambio de energia positiva y con amor* ... An *even* exchange of energy, *positive and with love*. When a communication truly comes from the heart, it includes an ingrained honesty wrapped in clarity, sincerity, and integrity.

Truth in Communications. While upbeat and positive communications serve their grand purposes, there can also be times when Egos are reluctant to hear the 'naked truth'. In either case, *heartful honesty spoken with kindness is key to binding together the Soul of a flourishing relationship.*

Take note of situations around you and look for yourself to see the powerful impact of the above ingredients when they are demonstrated in alignment!

Is Patience optional, when convenient, or is it mandatory for a flourishing relationship? Clearly, *the practice of patience* in relationship contributes so immensely to this core foundation, being *another essential part of the glue that holds it all together.* By now, having read and internalized the previous Chapters of this Book, this Truth should be obvious to you and of no surprise!

You are wise from this moment forward to consider patience as mandatory and not optional!

Open lines of Communication

Erode or cut quality communications, and you plague the relationship. There is no polite way to say this, nor an excuse that will bolster neglect in communications!

As Benjamin Franklin was quoted in this Book's Chapter on CHANGE, a similar phrase would do him honor, by simply saying:

When you are finished with <u>communication</u>, you are finished!

Now, let Us mention *certain* communications, those subject to *Divine Timing*.

If timing <u>demands</u> are unduly rushed to suit 'other schedules', by an Ego insisting *upon having its way, ... that way is often out of sync with the Universe and the natural flow of energy.* Have you noticed any consequences of this?

At other times, an <u>Ego demand</u> for the Universe to perform *will typically result in Divine silence and without response.* This has been called crowding Spirit!

Delivery

Talking fast and using incomplete, fractured sentences and thoughts has become a *vogue behavioral standard of certain generations upcoming* on your Earth plane, GenX and other younger generational mutations in particular. If this be your generation: Nota Bene, Dear Friends! Slow down, take your time, and make communications and enunciation abundantly clear, so it counts!

Have you noticed breakdowns that result from communication inadequacies? Leadership is truly needed in untangling this maelstrom of your governmental, societal, educational, and personal mix-ups. The lot could surely use your Mastered skills to assist in aligning this confusion for All Humanity. *Consider what part you could play in contributing to the greater good of literacy and Human communication?*

"Put ambiguity aside, Dear Ones, and make your communication clear, crisp, and well considered before your mouth shall otherwise have its way."

Generational failure about learning to read and write script handwriting is also a <u>communication, educational and literacy breakdown of unthinkable proportions.</u> Consider that reading and writing of handwriting is prominent upon your Earth. Despite the unprecedented invasion of digital technology, handwriting script is commonly <u>and</u> easily used with many of your Earth Languages. **Encourage and Teach your younger generations to learn, and do them this great favor, in spite of the educational systems and <u>lazy generational resistance that lingers.</u> <u>You can learn,</u> if this applies to you!**

Breakdowns in Communication

<u>Undelivered communications</u> are one of three major catagories of UPSETS, as explained in the Self-Love Chapter of this book. Do you remember?

When information is withheld, or when it is disguised and/or partially delivered, either way, it is undelivered and a common cause of Upsets. Also, remember the ghosting factor of communications, where a relationship partner refuses to talk about an important issue, or just simply cuts off communication altogether and the glue disappears.

An underlying part of any healthy relationship is communication, <u>alive and well</u>. When this is cut off, a major breakdown is set to occur, perhaps quickly, and you may soon be turning to the Detachment and Moving-On Chapters of this book before you know it!

Where is Patience in all of this? Find out 'what happened' when you finally catch up with your partner, about any withholds or possible accountability issues ... until you have all of facts and the scenario. Maybe something was out of his or her control? Once you have the full picture, there can be compassion for circumstances, and maybe not?... along with a clearing and moving forward together.

Be aware that <u>Passive-aggressive communication behavior between partners</u> is a devastating blow, and could *need serious repair and damage control as a result! Not to mention a needed rebuilding of TRUST with the partner who is passive-aggressive.*

Passive-Aggressive Behavior, *from a psychological standpoint* is characterized by a habitual pattern of non-active resistance to *expected agreements*, injecting opposition, sullenness, stubbornness, and negative attitudes in response to requirements for normal, or <u>agreed upon</u>, performance levels.

It also frequently occurs in workplace relationships, where resistance is exhibited by indirect/oblique behaviors as <u>procrastination, misplaced priorities, willful omissions, broken promises, forgetfulness, and purposeful inefficiency</u>, and at times <u>in reaction to demands by authority figures.</u>

Reestablishing Broken Trust

In a sense, there becomes a need for 'starting all over'. This is akin to reaffirming your vows ... <u>about recommitting to agreements on fundamentals, common purposes, promises, and heart-related feelings between partners</u> ... that must be reestablished in good faith, to set things straight and be able to move on in harmony and higher vibration, ... as <u>before</u> the passive-aggressive actions occurred. **Consider this a renewal of your shared vows!**

This said, with rapid speed electronic devices and your Internet with its tools, there is little excuse for partners being completely out of touch for extended ghosting periods!

Avoiding carelessness. Consciously putting love and care into the timing, content, and vibrations of your communications **will pay off many fold in enhancing the quality of a relationship that has true meaning to you.**

Otherwise, carelessness will have its way, sometimes escalating to injured feelings, dysfunction, and often chaos.

About Rushing Communications

Have you heard the old saying …

"We are in such a hurry, and yet …. if the result is flawed, we ALWAYS have time to do it over again!" Author unknown.   And possibly need to untangle things!

Take your time and get it correct the *first time* around!

An antidote, you ask? *Careful thought, consideration,* **and focused attention on your communications**, verbal, written, electronic, etc., *can help you to slow down a bit and get it 'right' , as you would say, the first time.*

Human Interactions. We have put forth to you in many channeled dissertations that progress in your relationships depends in a great part upon your learning to polish up skills of Human emotional *interactions.* As you advance, these skills you acquire will include synchronizing events between your partner(s), individuals, groups, institutions ... a wide variation of personalities ... and as the interplay of emotions and communication takes effect.

Skillful, *well-considered communications* will intermesh synchronously, with great harmony, effectiveness, and without great effort on your part.

With some reflection, it will become apparent that your *personal relationship communications involve a transfer of delicate energy from one Being to another.*

The quality of communication is controlled the way you package it for transit ... <u>the way you wrap the energy</u> with an intention, love, emotion, etc. It is Your choice and your responsibility!

> Building Trust in your Communications requires attention to your choice of words and focus upon their delivery and then ... insuring that your actions match up with your communication!

You can be Master of clear communications or let your communications breakdowns be the Master of you.

Worthy of mention, as We close this Chapter, is to learn to communicate in <u>a way that can be heard and understood. Remember, there is the Receiver of your transmissions who needs your consideration!</u>

*Call it effective communication. We, for example, in this transmission, are writing in a style to reach a wide audience of Earthly receivers, **and** also to include those advancing to higher levels in Practical Spirituality.*

Spirit Intends that Your Relationships be pleasant, effective, emotionally balanced, and serving your highest aligned purpose with honor.

One of the *faces of You* turns out to be the way you communicate.

Included in the Heightened Vibrations of communication, are those *housed in your voice and body.* *These are of gargantuan importance to success in the Grand Process of your Mastery. Now is your chance to learn, to practice, and to shine as a true Master of Communicators. You are born to shine, Dear Ones!*

𝓑lessings along your Journey,

Saint Germain

Though Lah Rahn Ananda aka Gordon Corwin II

Chapter 12

Creating Space for 'Us' and 'We'

"Joy is not in things, it is in us".
Benjamin Franklin

The heartbeat of relationship is located at this core … where the 'Us and the We' comes into Being as One. *This union is the GLUE that creates the space of unity and holds 'US' together away from separateness of only the 'I' identity.*

As surely as individuals make up a partnership in union, they can maintain their own appropriate identities as well with synchronicity. We have pointed out earlier where various factors contribute energy and power to the mix of Us and We. Consider mutual aspirations, shared visions, needs, shared pleasures, common goals, mutual respect, and more. If certain factors are in Divine alignment, all the better, such as Soul partners, kindred Spirits or friends now reunited in their Spiritual Journeys.

*The point here is about **the intention of relationship** being highly synergistic, positive, productive, healthy and pleasant, if not highly pleasurable. Meaning that the creation and Being of the Us and the WE bound together and functioning in harmony will <u>exponentially</u> outstrip the sum of the individual parts (partners) acting separately.*

In order to step into the full mindset of US and WE, a sincere student of relationships needs to gain experience in applying the fundamentals Spirit presents to you, in preceding chapters on: Discovering Triggers, Change,

Forgiveness, Emotions, Self-talk, Patience, Self-love and Communication. Before you proceed here, you will be wise to review so you can be ready for the payoffs that follow!

Learning. *It is good to remember, that as Humans, you often need to intake information, spoken, written, visual and otherwise, ... at least three (3) times to fully comprehend <u>and</u> connect the dots! Surprising?*

*T**o mention briefly, ... a note about caring for the 'Well Being' of US and We.* This union of energies, is *ideally nourished and equally cared for by the partners.* We speak in particular about *mutual consideration of each other* as Human Beings shouldering their own individual challenges as they blaze their own trail in their journey. ... along with simultaneously engaging in relationship as a committed partner.

Persevering and building the Us and the We requires a special dedication to the mutual goals, visions, desires and needs of the 'relationship' to function in harmony with ease and grace. *Heartfully caring for one another is an attribute* of partners that We see to be an essential ingredient in the cohesive glue We speak about.

However, through neglect and careless self-indulgent behavior, relationship can sadly crumble and totally be obliterated by a partner(s) who descends into weakness and wretchedness allowing arrogance and selfishness to corrupt this otherwise beautiful bonding in reality! We shall directly speak to you here about Narcissism as behavior that can subtly creep in or expand before it is discovered and addressed! Focusing on Our guidelines will greatly increase your chances of preserving and augmenting a relationship to be healthy, alive and well!

What about Balance? *Instinctively or by agreement, balance contributes so heavily to the Us and We. While* <u>one</u> *partner may input large amounts of love and caring energies, there is a need for* <u>balance in this energy</u> <u>exchange.</u> *This must be respected by the other partner(s), delivering a reasonable energy contribution in- kind, (pun intended).* A partner's Behavior showing <u>indifference and neglect</u> in this balance will soon cripple and bring a relationship to its knees.

Balancing energies of contribution *maintains an awareness of action in the moment, such that either partner could easily assume and/or switch roles between the 'giver'*

or to the 'taker' and vice versa, back and forth with love, generosity, ease and grace. The golden glue is now flowing freely, do you see? There is an extreme fulfillment of heart-warming satisfaction when you create the dynamic of giving and receiving in pure joy, <u>without reservation</u>, quid pro quo, nor selfishness nor greed anywhere in sight!

As spoken in the Chapter of Self-Love, "This means, Folks, that *from the start of this union, as a relationship candidate, you are obliged to erase any traces of* **'Narcissism'** *that any Partner's Ego, including thyself, may hold sacred and/or demand in the flow of your relationship.*

If these patterns or even traces of 'I alone' be yours or your partners, you must correct and <u>elevate this pattern into a Self-love vibration in order to open the</u>

'Your Ego can hold you captive in its prison if you choose to be shackled there, *but know that if you allow this, Self-love shall not be yours!* **A high price, indeed it is, for a Human Spirit of potential to pay for the stubborn and resolute self-indulgences of Narcissism!'**

gates of US and We, leading to a true relationship foundation!

As an aside, since love can contribute wonderfully to relationships of all sorts, *consider for a moment the opposing dark force resident in a plane of Duality such as your Planet Earth. For example, if a narcissistic relationship partner (or candidate partner) is indeed incapable of Love, your conclusion may indeed be tempered by guidance We offer in 'Approaching Relationship' or in 'Moving On'. Realistic food for meditation?*

Denial. We Above often see denial as a behavior pattern in relationships, where Self-love has not been fully ingrained, and a desperate clinging and hanging on then prevails ... until the denial is transmuted into conscious choice, which then faces the reality at hand. When Truth surfaces, however, partners have regenerative opportunities to change and grow together, *creating Win-Win solutions for attracting Light into the mix, if that be the choice that wins out! Let Us pray that Love prevails leading to and sustaining an aligned Divine outcome, Folks.*

Win-Win. You may recall a song lyric in your time, written by a famous performer who valued the quality of life and relationship harmony. The lyric points to the all-important *Win-Win philosophy* by simply saying **that nobody wins unless everyone wins!** Contrary to common and predominant Human behavior in your World, _adopting the Win-Win philosophy in your life will open a magnificent space in your Being,_ a place that most Humans stubbornly fail to enter as they fully subscribe to and are trapped into living relationships guided by your _Earthly Duality_! Be Extraordinary and transcend behavior of the masses Folks! This is your time to shine and set the example!

ぴゃ

We spoke earlier about Self-love. When you walk through the gates of Self-Love, focusing on Love and Light as being joyfully yours, you will be delighted to share your fulfillment with an openness that _gives a special space to an abundance of Us and We in unison._

Let Us now focus on the Light as a Love attraction that can allow lasting passions of various types to flow between partners of all types.

In _various relationships,_ and involving various sizes and shapes of partners, even unromantic, there can be a magical ingredient called LOVE, believe it or not! Love has many faces. When LOVE is born into Being in a relationship, a **tolerance and empathy _shows up_ between**

the partners that smooths out many of the little wrinkles and speedbumps that arise.
     Give and take on minor issues can then more naturally evolve, and believe it or not, be *occasionally humorous in retrospect!* Present this cohesive ingredient of Love, … constant fears, annoyance and confrontations that muddy the waters can soon drift away!

     So, with the 'Us and We' solidly in place at this time, We Ascended give you a next section entitled:

Focusing Your Spiritual Journey.

Here, We repeat some earlier words leading you deeply into this focus of your Spiritual Journey, *The Triangle of Love,* to open your heart to new possibilities that would transcend. Truly focused, this joyful energy that becomes a part of your Being, is yours for the taking, now and forever. A higher vibration capable of sustaining LOVE is waiting in the wings to meld into your automatic way of Being … if you are willing. *Holding a sustained vibration of Love,* overall in your Being, or an intermittent and lesser level, something lower, limited by specific circumstances, *is your choice as you climb different rungs of the Spiritual ladder. Unconditional Love is the flavor of the top rung in the Spiritual ladder,* one that We Ascended hold on your behalf, joined as one energy in the Heavens above you, as you read.

> *Relationship Mastery requires discovering those default responses, packed tightly in your belief system, that will surely need to be jettisoned while Ego must pay the price!*

This purity spans your cells and chakras, entwining you in its magic spell.
Such Love is simply *present*. No thought, premeditation, rehearsal, or effort is in any *part of this phenomenon.*

> We understand, at times, what a painful process this can be, *when Truth is uncovered, ... to maintain the Love vibration.* This is the Ego price that must be paid, Dear Friends. Choose as your free-will chooses, We do not interfere in this process. It is the Law. Ascended Spirit, as enlightened Ambassadors of God, *offers you options of choice.*
> As many of you are already aware, Love has many facets and faces. There are many ways to Love and be in Alignment.

<u>Throughout your Grand Process</u>, consciously raising your Spiritual vibration within your whole Being, **allows you to be drawn closer and closer by the hand of God and Spirit. Divine reciprocity is truly magical, Dear Friends. Gift yourself to recognize and savor the feeling in your Earthly real time when next you are held in Love's magic spell.**

> *Love has many facets and faces. Overall, the aim of Our Divine gift is to source you to be Loveable and to Love! Reaching and holding this vibration is your key to Being in this magnificent room of joy, peace, and bliss.*

∽∂

For experienced relationship partners, the ' We' and 'US' mindset is a given. It is a natural space that comes easily to you and needs little coaxing or attention. Whereas for other relationship participants, *the 'We' and 'Us' mindset is new, sometimes very strange and foreign, sometimes an unfamiliar way to think and Be.*

Ones who have traditionally thought in <u>solo terms of 'Me' and 'I'</u> will need some TLC to adapt and make the shift. Here again, comes CHANGE. If TLC is needed, let this be an <u>open topic among</u> partners. With practice and heartful commitment, the change can occur in an amazingly short time. It's team work time now! And yes, <u>shared control</u> can easily be addressed, considering the best use of different strengths each partner brings to the table, without compromising the integrated <u>latitude for individuality</u> of creative contributions.

∽∂

Relationship partners who tend toward the Narcissistic are <u>very deeply challenged</u> to implement this change process, as it could mean a substantial <u>rewiring of a belief system</u> to become a harmonious partner! **Narcissism is defined in your Earth World "as an inordinate fascination with oneself, excessive vanity, self-centeredness, selfishness and egocentrism; an <u>infantile</u> level of personality development."** *Various degrees of self-centeredness, selfishness and arrogance* could play a devastating part in your relationship, if not recognized, nipped in the bud, or eliminated! Perhaps individual professional counseling is required to dissolve the resistance patterns that would stand in the way of someone being on the team?

If this be true, *let it come out early in the formation stage of a relationship, rather than be discovered down the road, as something well disguised in the beginning. We have already spoken to you about Approaching and decisions made.* See: <u>Approaching Your Relationships</u> Chapter in this book.

∽∂

Operating in the Us and We mindset using a healthy practice of <u>shared control</u>.

With mutual goals and certain capabilities of relationship partners clearly in mind, shared control is a natural way to reach agreements, with Trust and confidence in place. Power struggles can erupt when shared control agreements are unclear or a subject of contention. Oversight here brings Ego confrontations that are easily avoided with <u>agreed upon shared control</u>, <u>up front and in place!</u> We encourage you to use this as an opportunity for increased efficiency and conservation of energy along with compatibility.

In the beginning and throughout a relationship, constructively balancing the exchange of energies between partners can be consciously initiated, using some common sense practices with each other, such as:

Agreement to support each other.

Agreeing to relate with enthusiasm, positive energy, and joy.

Mutually recognizing *boundaries* of the other and one's self.

Respecting agreements upon the roles of Partners and their defined scope(s) of work.

Focusing together, with priority, on pertinent issues, not the minutia.

Distinctly recognizing Needs and Wants.

Being flexible on the small stuff.

Agreeing to show *consideration to each other.*

Making requests versus demands.

Agreeing to give personal Space - to learn and grow together without smothering.

Openly communicating, without withholds.

Offering more observations and fewer 'opinions'.

Celebrate together!! Victories, Togetherness, and Differences.

Learning to accept the Downs as well as the Ups.

Three Faces of Appreciation. Working together is **nourished greatly** by showing appreciation, one partner to another. A cheerful thank you, in a sense. But in Truth, what is the real message underneath?

We would like to refine this energy of appreciation, so you can be clear about what you or a partner are really appreciating when you say 'I appreciate it'.

It can mean: I appreciate *getting what I want* (leaving out the person),

It can mean: I appreciate *YOU as a person*, getting me what I want,

Or it can mean: I both appreciate You as a person and I appreciate getting what I want.

We observe that relationship partners, sometimes taking the other for granted, can fall into this trap, *leaving out the 'You'* in favor of the 'I', and sending out that naked intention or energy in their message.

Feelings are real between the most seasoned of relationship partners, and *being truly appreciated* counts high on the list of ingredients of the Glue that holds everything together and makes a partnership endure!

Connecting the Dots ... Win-Win solutions <u>and</u> The Power of 'US'.

> *The <u>'compromise'</u>, as a well-worn out solution, is so common in your World, yet so deeply impregnated with an Earth-World consciousness that buys the Human Illusion as its flawed truth.*

Let's focus briefly here on *compromise* **with respect to relationship.** *Differences of opinion and of firm belief system convictions often appear in a relationship. These are, for example, some individually sourced interpretations, in varying perspectives of merit that can cause friction and discord.*

***Abrasive situations**, as you must know by now, can be handled with the partners in ways such as <u>directly talking it out and agreeing</u>, or <u>amicably and positively clearing the issue with</u> no remnants, or <u>ignoring and letting it stack up</u> on top of all the other issues, yet unresolved (sweeping one more unresolved issue under the carpet), etc..* So take a turn on clarifying *what needs to be purged* from your relationship, and what alternative **Win-Win solutions** you can create to erase the friction and ultimately forward the mutually aligned purpose.

An Open Willingness to Communicate in Truth, *of course, is <u>mandatory and axiomatic</u> for a True Relationship to flourish. With the portal of open communications in place, We now have the makings of <u>eligibility for a Win-Win solution</u>! The Chapter of this Book - 'Communications' -*

elaborates upon this mandatory ingredient of Glue holding relationships together, intact and healthy.

Know that a mere compromise brings elements to the table which commonly satisfy <u>some</u> of the needs/wants/requests of each partner, **But often leaves out**, by definition, other parts wanted or needed or requested by the party(s).

So where does that leave the relationship partners about being supported and satisfied about attitudes and moves in an effort to continue in harmony toward mutual goals?

Being left dissatisfied or in emotional limbo casts its own shadow on the compromise just reached, even though 'agreed' upon.

Full-hearted agreement, surrender, acceptance, good faith and detachment *may hold a compromise in place in the moment* … and then again, will it be lasting? Would you like to know about a Divinely sourced solution that transcends compromise? Read on, Dear Ones.

∽ ∾

Now **We come to the heart of the matter**, Connecting the Dots … Win-Win solutions AND The Power of 'US'.

Spirit highly endorses a fresh approach for many. (Acknowledgment and recognition is due to introspective designers who specialize in tailoring their products to be customer friendly **and** simultaneously benefit **the offering organization, demonstrating a Win-Win philosophy).**

When relationship issues surface, We suggest approaching with a quiet mind, a pause and break if needed, and then a considered reply in place of the tempting knee-jerk reactive response with emotions spinning out of control and escalating more complications into the mix.

At these very moments in your interactions are the Golden Opportunities for searching out a Win-Win solution(s) with your partner.

'Alright, let's talk about this for a moment before we make any moves'.

'What are some perspectives and alternatives WE (partners together) can create now to turn this around into a Win-Win?*'*

You both (all involved) will be surprised at the solutions that will pop up out of nowhere, emerge into possibility, be suggested by Spirit, or come from your own intuitions, individual or collective. Look for the answers that are hiding from you in plain sight. Answers, floating in from right brain activity that you are *unaccustomed to accessing,* and nonetheless, … here they are, ready to be proposed!

> *If you can access the Power of Your Higher-self and bypass nagging Ego forces that invade, Win-Win solutions can be found as your saving grace.*

This will take some practice, as ingrained habits are not easily broken. Practice *'O.K., (partner) let's look for the Win-Win here, recognize it, agree to it, and off we go!*

Beware of the NIH Syndrome that prevails among many creative minds. *'Not Invented Here, No Good'* is an Ego sourced mantra that is played over in many minds wrestling for self-esteem versus the optimum Win-Win solution for the highest good. Thinkers Nota Bene!

Alright, Folks. Wasn't that easier than you expected when you began reading about **Connecting the Dots ... Win-Win solutions AND The Power of 'US'?**

Many Blessings to you all. Apply these solutions and witness a gargantuan leap forward in the elevation of your individual consciousness, your relationship itself, and your overall life-stream alignment with the harmony of your Soul, Spirit and the Universe.

Manifestation Cronies:
Capability and Willingness, or Both?

As partners may contribute to a relationship in their own unique ways, there nonetheless lies some turf that needs to be replowed and consequently needs to be seen from a fresh, clear viewpoint. We are speaking of the distinction, in reference to a partner, having 'Capability' versus 'Willingness', as cronies that would ideally function together in sync.

Surely, relationship partners have certain capabilities, some valuable resources that he/she brings to the party. Hopefully partners bring in a diversity of talents along with mutual aspirations and goals. Hence shared control agreements. However, *resistance can separate these capabilities from actually being used ... as in 'willingness'. Passive-aggressive resistance* to satisfy an Ego desire, or outright uncooperative actions emanating from a belief system packed with opinions resisting reality or change, or disregard for existing agreements, etc. can be a major partnership upset to be reckoned with. Keep in mind that a *Clearing between partners* can shed new Light on such a deadlock, if this willingness can be brought into the mix.

On the other side lies *compassion for a partner who is totally willing,* and has not the capability to handle the manifestation at hand. Perhaps it is uncovered that a partner is being required to perform a feat that is beyond his capability. Here, aptitude, inexperience, naïveté, unawareness, and other factors would suggest needed training, counseling, perhaps coaching to come up to speed and match up capability with a wonderful ready and able willingness of that partner to fill a role!

Love the Journey!

It is yours to Own!

As you blend together your individual energies into those of Us and We, notice the interplay of the yin and yang within, and also with your partner(s) in Relationship. Delicately handled, these collective energies can add great strength to the GLUE that bonds your partnership in a space of unity.

Rely then, upon the power of *enlightened* teamwork and bonding through this mindset of Us and We as trustable assets to anchor your relationships of all types.

With Love and Affection, I send My Blessings to you.

Saint Germain

Through Lah Rahn Ananda aka Gordon Corwin II

Chapter 13

Perspectives About 'We and Me'

Now that I have Divinely guided you thus far about Relationship Dynamics, another very important distinction must be seeded and grown within your consciousness, at this juncture. That would be to consciously hold in your heart the Oneness of your Relationship, allowing the tethers of Love and a deep level friendship. These energies can then be *simultaneously placed in tune with the aligned priorities of your Personal Universe coupled with Spirit as the <u>Centerpiece</u>*.

Alright! As you are entering into the *space* We *have just described above, you are ready for the next step forward into the realm of COURAGE!*

When you *authentically* summon the pure COURAGE to open a new pathway pattern for yourself, abandoning the EGO's firm grip and stance of supremacy, the effects of upset and resistance can noticeably subside and can soon vanish into the ethers ... as you gain true perspective of *You, Me and We*, all integrated in Relationship in this phase.

We teach students of Spirit, Truth seekers, and Light Carriers to seek out NEW PERSPECTIVES as *they contemplate and view and* observe *Earthly events, circumstances, emotions, and interactions of relationship ... that penetrate a life-stream and give cause for questioning.*

As you contemplate perspectives, *have you ever considered Lord Chief Joseph's sage advice to "*stand in the other man's shoes, feel what he may be feeling, and look back at yourself, standing in your own shoes*"? Try it sometime! Let Me know how it works out for you!*

Many find that this standing in the other man's shoes process *opens portals, some of which are internal to the Chelas own heart chakra energies, that may need to be cleared. Once fully cleared at all levels,* new perspectives and solutions are known to joyfully pop up in a spontaneous and magical time of inspiration.

Backing off from the magnifying glass approach, *where little details can cloud the issue, and standing where you can see the BIG PICTURE, ... will enormously assist your EGO in surrendering to achieve completions of your Upsets and restore you to the highest level of vibration you can muster, ... at this point of your evolvement.*

As I travel with you through this sensitive territory, be fully aware of the irony that beholds. Then observe the absolute Truths of the polar opposites involved in *living the balanced perspectives to follow*.

Given the deep loyalty, Love, affection, and devotion that can accompany relationship, a need for *individuation* also raises its head for recognition. In the previous Chapter 4, Self-love on page 56, you saw a certain Diagram, do you remember? Now that you have traveled along to this point, the following very same diagram to follow may have a deeper meaning to you?

To Repeat, ...

Let Me now briefly state a paramount, gigantic point of Truth, enabling you to elevate and sustain your Relationships of all types. Alright! *Your ultimate success in creating and sustaining loving, Self-loving, and satisfying Relationships depends greatly upon your Free-will Choices to adequately blend the Boundaries of your consciousness!*

There is a *delicate balance* in play here, to respect the boundary itself, and yet to simultaneously *blend* that boundary(s) with the adjacent boundary. From the below diagram, focus for now upon the ME and WE boundaries, and visualize how you can adequately balance and connect these energies into Oneness ... in place of *abrupt separation*. This Balance is yours to create, Dear Ones!

This pictorial *overlap of consciousnesses* shows a synchronous blending of energies that is needed for a true relationship to be born, blossom, and thrive.

Blending of Consciousness

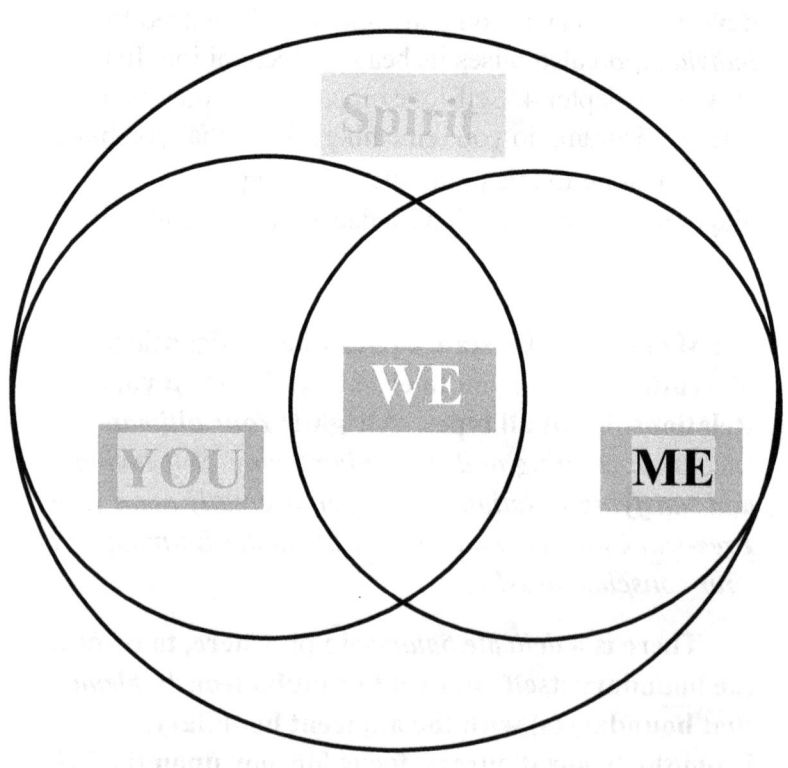

And now for the irony. We in Spirit have guided you to recognize the beauty and wholeness of your relationship in a 'We and Me' context, and still to hold sacred a part of you that adores Spirit and maintains Self-Love intact. We in Spirit have discussed this many times previously.

Here now, *for your expanded perspective*, is the bottom line: Visualize your personal Universe partnered *with Spirit as the* highest *centerpiece of your Earth-life as you seek to evolve into the Light. Notice that the We relationship overlaps and yet is distinct from You and Me, and is included as part of the entire circle* of your personal Universe. And ... yes, all are Loved, cherished, and often adored ... in Perspective.

The 'You, Me and We' *are what they are, held in Love at a grand level, and yet these are parts of the whole. Are you with me? Imagine simultaneous Loves, if you will! Recognize the relationship (Master chuckles ...haaaa ha) of set and subset, for you mathematical geniuses on the rise!*

Mastering these relationship parts surely stands elevated in the ranks of life lessons that massage those pieces of you that need to be polished up to a high gloss, ... higher parts *outreaching energies of Ego and those dull coping mechanisms that would* seem *to suffice for the day.*

Imbedded in relationship experiences are certain tests and hurdles that can be challenging, indeed. Here I begin to address one such challenge that vexes many of you and can sink your ship ... if you are not on your toes and alert. This would be... ***Attachments!***

Insights about Attachment and Detachment

To impart some clarity, I shall give you some definitions in broad terms. *Exactly what are Attachments to which I refer?*

Attachments are a mindset of behaviors and emotions to which a Human Ego clings and grasps tightly, ...*in a desperate effort to establish permanence over the temporary, to be right, to selfishly win, to avoid consequences of change, and a host of other motivations. Humans can become attached to a long list that can include people, beliefs and opinions, ideas, outcomes, money, material items, religions and, yes indeed, relationships! Attachments often carry an illusionary intention of 'everlasting and forever permanent'.*

Thus far, life experience has no doubt shown that when you venture into close relationship, you face the attractions of Attachment. *Ones churning in the heat of it all are usually oblivious to being attached until they are, and easily overlook the reality of effects surrounding their feelings and actions while Attached.* Consequently, We see from Above that many have surrendered their power and energy, sometimes to another(s), to *becoming hopelessly attached and strangely obsessed and dominated by their own self-created clingings to fill various Ego wants and fears of loss!* A high Attachment price to pay for Soul Freedom lost!

Also especially high is the price of pain and suffering along the way that stem from the root cause of Attachment. Have you read the Buddha?

Actually, pain happens when reality does not coincide with the things and beliefs you are attached to!
Illusion and self-deception therefore play a lead role on this stage, with you as the leading actor.
Ponder this irony for a moment, ... energy well spent and worthy of your time at this juncture.
Uncover the Ego parts that hold you captive in self-deception, delusion, and separate from reality, <u>including the permanence of Human life itself (and of relationships, included by default)</u>.

Can you clearly see the irony within Attachments, *which carry the illusion of a behavior that would bind Love, caring, and devotion, etc. and yet through this indulgence would deliver that very outcome of pain and suffering that you are attempting to avoid? Ponder this for some moments, before you proceed.*

> *As you evolve into a new state of mind apart from blatant Attachment that Binds, ... you create the Freedom for now choosing to embrace Detachment with Love, ... and to realize that this evolved vibration is not a lowered compromise of affection or loyalty, but rather an upward intensification of realigned and balanced Beingness!*

Also, hold clearly in your awareness that moving into Detachment with Love is a heightened state of mind held in <u>true</u> Perspective of Us and Me, and not a compromise position, nor a 'bandage' as you might say, concealing an ongoing Attachment wound waiting to be healed!

Read on, My Dear Ones, and allow the light of Spirit to illuminate My words for your understanding, opening space beyond mere understanding for your knowing and living of this Wisdom.

❦

Can you now see that indulging in Attachments that inextricably Bind and in Judgments outside of Observation … are both Ego behaviors that ultimately self-inflict wounds with consequences in your quality of Earth life? Alright, and there is more!

I rarely, if ever, reveal the gravity of Attachment tied to the Karmic Wheel. So this may be a first in some eons. Human Attachments have *multidimensional consequences* as I reveal in this dissertation. So here you are!

Certain attachments are born from Ego that would hold you in separation <u>from Reality and Truth</u> as distinct <u>from illusion</u>. Chelas with awareness soon learn from initiations to *trade* their illusions of Attachments that bind for Truth and Reality that empowers. They are amazed and overjoyed with the Freedom they Self-create!

Know that strong unbreakable Attachments to certain <u>Wants</u>, out of perspective, are driven by strong Ego behaviors in action. *This choice will keep you inextricably stuck in your seat on the Karmic Wheel.*

Moving on ... Attachments ... can easily morph into obsessive behaviors, <u>tying Humans to the very Earthly connections that, ironically, must be released to be truly Free,</u> allowing Ones to transition, and perhaps Ascend, ... out of the 3rd dimension and into the 4th and 5th and higher Dimensions of Consciousness.

Note that certain attachments can be further reinforced by *addiction.* **Remember that transcending Ego-sourced behaviors is an axiomatic** part of the Grand Process,

Without this *fundamental wisdom in place and in action*, you block your own needed openings to truly walk your path, aligned with your dharma, and to realize milestones of progress in your Spiritual Journey! *You would be wise at this point to also intake further wisdom on processing and transmuting emotions by reading* The Saint Germain Chronicles Collection, Lah Rahn Ananda aka Gordon Corwin II, Amazon, 2016.

I hasten to add that Spiritually responsible living is also axiomatic here for progress. Releasing Attachments *is in no way to be confused with erroneous permissions to dishonor integrity nor your responsibilities and agreements of living in harmony! As we proceed, your*

upholding Spiritual Law, Universal Law, and Human agreements <u>all support Order</u>, the first Law of the Divine.

'Exercise Temperance with Attachments …

now you know … indulgence has a Cost'.

❦

Overcoming indulgence in **Attachment and engaging in Detachment in Love** offer a relaxed hand that still Loves and cares, eliminating a forceful binding and gripping that promises illusionary rewards. You may yourself observe the illusion of Attachment, as it tempts and offers juicy momentary satisfaction, feelings of security, permanence, and 'success', a way to *permanently* hold on or be held, opportunity to dominate or be dominated, etc.

Forceful binding <u>opposes</u> an available fresh and relaxed approach to Relationship that would bring ease and grace. On the contrary, **Naked Attachment** that binds will produce consequences, painful when the day of reckoning raises its head! Trust Me, We in the Realm observe from Above countless *outcomes of Attachment that stray far and wide <u>from intended outcomes</u> of Attachees!* These Ones regularly pray to Us Above to be exonerated from consequences of their free-will actions. Oh My!

You are about to witness the unbridled disrobing and full exposure of Attachments per se, once and for

all, and you shall see the Truth beneath the veil, … ahhh yes. (Master chuckles Ha Haaa.)

Examine some of your major Attachments, and notice the congruity of My words with the energy that flows around *your* Attachments at this very moment.

*** In your personal observations, know this: *If you can willingly release with ease and grace for the higher good, … that to which you are Attached, … you are freed, … and are experiencing Detachment with Love!*

As you read further, look for My words and energies comparing *Attachments of Want to Attachments of Need, a distinction fundamental to your journey here.*

Many motivations surround Attachment, and you must fill in the blanks about your own motivations, fears, urges, desires, beliefs, opinions, etc. (including *your own illusions* if you Be advanced enough to detect them?) … which comprise part of your 'small story'. Such behaviors can skew the *perspective* We bring forth here, *clouding the Big story* that is dear to your happiness, progress, and evolution and Freedom! *Self-awareness of your motivations* will accelerate your progress.

Devote time and energy to their discovery, as uncovering will reward you with an expanded awareness, and rewards of relief. Otherwise observe the pain and suffering that Attachment ultimately brings to your life, blocking your door to Freedom. Can you connect the dots?

You may have discerned by now that this process is for the courageous and not for the faint of heart, avoiding Truth and Reality. A conscious effort over months and sometimes even years of Earth time will be *needed to instill and maintain the practice of **Detachment in Love** into your automatic daily behaviors* that deliver the Freedom you seek! Nota Bene, and enjoy the rewards of persistence and self-dedication to your evolution. **I** will commend you when you cross finish lines of Attachment Mastery!

☙❧

For those with courage to face and Master their Attachments <u>without denial,</u> I would inject here some distinctions that will serve you well.

Attachments of Need, and Attachments of Want. At the outset, We recognize that fuzzy or grey lines can appear, showing that binary black or white requires intuitive license when distinguishing Needs from Wants. In individual cases, there are exceptions that surface and may cross certain lines. However, the *main objective of clarity, remains nonetheless, firmly visible!*

Attachments to healthy Needs are held nicely in the Human consciousness satisfying *autonomic needs, plus necessary urges and habits to sustain the <u>healthy life of ease without disease.</u>* Spirit is surely in agreement! Your own list of needs will likely include air to breathe, shelter, water, food to nourish, suitable activity, social contact, sexual release, self-Love, Love of Spirit, and other *appropriate essentials of need to support Human fundamentals to live an aligned life in balance.*

Living Habits. I note for you in this context that those life habits of Need, which support your highest good are indeed commendable, and clearly separate from *the habits of Want* and *Attachment to Wants that can bind you to the 3rd Dimensional energies of your Earth-World.* Dedication to healthy habits of need for your highest good is in full support of your Personal Universe.

ॐ

Now comes **Attachment to Wants. Be clear about this distinction**, as We observe many Humans are *gigantically confused as you label Wants as being Needs. Many of you justify Wants as Needs*, in denial of your higher-self Truth that knows better!

So, for your own growth, it would be well to list, here and now, your Truthful version of your **Wants, separate from Needs.**
With this clarity, you can venture forth in *the game of releasing Ego driven Attachments to fulfillment of Wants, binding you tightly to the 3rd Dimension that you wish to leave behind you!*

My Wants as of (date)_____.

_____
_____
_____
_____
_____
_____

_____
_____
_____
_____
_____
_____
_____
_____
_____
_____

Addiction to Wants can further reinforce their permanence … if not brought to the surface and consciously addressed without typical Human denial, justification, excuses, or arguments! *Some in your World describe Addictions as 'Attachments Gone Mad'.*

We note that many, many Human addictions to Wants remain firmly in place on your Plane.

Test yourself as you proceed, My Dear Ones. An easy self-test of your Attachment and/or possible addiction to an Attachment to is to Truthfully ask yourself: "Am I freely willing to release this want of mine for the well-being or betterment of Myself or Others?

Let me be clear. It is Attachment to <u>feeding your energy into pursuit of Ego bound Earthly Wants and trivia of which I speak of at this point.</u>

Here is your opportunity to expose those possible or clear <u>*addictions to Attachments*</u> *that surround your life at this time.* Yes, if you are <u>Truthful</u> to yourself, some addictions will seem *just too personal* and difficult to admit, possibly embarrassing. If you wish to make progress, include these in your list without hesitation. Your list can be private.

Remember, outside of your comfort zone lies the real gold you can mine here with constructive change! Once visible and *above the surface*, these particulars will be on your radar and ready for Mastery processing!

<u>**The short list of Attachment wants can include primary desires**</u> <u>**for money, sex and power**</u>.

<u>**The long Attachment list**</u> **is one We often see from Humans today and throughout Human history. It includes a myriad of Wants, ... some you will recognize, perhaps?** *They commonly include always being right, obsession with the desire for excess money, denial, excess eating, over drinking, indulging as a habit, satisfying cravings (often at a large personal cost), excessive sexual activity or excessive abstinence, addiction to dominating, to being dominated or to not being dominated, addiction relationships overrunning your entire life, dependency, avoiding relationships, ... and the list is long. What is important here is YOUR list:*

Here and now it is your turn, Dear Friends, … to write **for your own reference** and progress record, and for further reflection and change, your: *addictions, near-addictions, and Attachments that you have. Be honest and Truthful with yourself, so this process will work!*

Addiction/Attachment   **Correction by When?**

_____
_____
_____
_____
_____
_____
_____
_____
_____
_____
_____
_____
_____
_____
_____
_____
_____
_____
_____
_____
_____
_____
_____
_____
_____
_____
_____

I support you in self-monitoring your progress bi-monthly, Folks. And, of course, you are welcome to report your progress and process to Me along the way. Observe where you are in this constructive change process. Bon Voyage!

ಶಿಖ

Releasing Ego Attachments. Having now identified Wants, Attachments, and Addictions to Attachments, I turn My energies, once again, toward process, toward *enlightening you about releasing Ego Attachments which bind you to the 3rd Dimensional Earth Plane.*

Ideally, when an Attachment is acknowledged 'for what it is', and along with reality minus drama, a Chela can then release it with ease and grace, leading to a peace of mind and a new Freedom.

Know well, as We begin this Releasing segment together, that Attachments or Addictions (Attachments gone Mad) that you allow in your life will hold you apart from turning Change into a friend in this lifetime.

Releasing is a process of redirecting of energies ... an altering of your state of mind. It is redirecting your energies to match up with Reality vs. allowing your

Ego behaviors, beliefs or opinions, those often harboring unmet expectations that cause frustration, disappointment, friction, and disillusionment ... to no longer prevail!

Release can be brought forth with ease and grace or *made as grueling as your free-will would choose.* As you begin to release Attachments, *notice your degree of willingness to evolve beyond your Earthly 3rd Dimension.*

Attachments, *supposedly released*, with lingering conditions of anger, regret, grudge, partial, temporary duration, excess sadness drama, etc. ... are waiting to *reappear and trigger further attachments* and emotions that can endure. We want forward progress for you, not relapse.

Sustaining your level of vibration is especially important *in experiencing enduring releases,* free from regret or emotional conditions that otherwise still cling and hold you prisoner. Be kind to yourself as you rewire this part of your consciousness. You may need some body work in the process. With higher vibration in place, you have cleared your path.

> **Look for *true* release. *A mere conditional release*, which your Ego would support, will dictate a return visit to your Attachment, guaranteed!**

Enter: **Detachment with Love.**

Here now is your marvelous opportunity to trade <u>Attachment with its Consequences</u> for <u>Detachment with Love,</u> ... *and to make this trade in alignment with all the dedication and enthusiastic <u>vigor and passion for life that you can muster.</u>*

Trading Attachment to beliefs, people, places, things ... for a mind-set of Detachment with Love ... is your Process.

This elevating transmutation of personal vibration within your Personal Universe holds you high above the pain and suffering *now relinquished to gain a priceless Freedom!*

In this state of Being, One's consciousness needs *aware free-will choice and re-choice in action to maintain and oft to grow the former levels of enthusiasm*, passion, inspiration, vision, engagement, caring and Love ... **as before the shift!**

Granted, this is a sensitive and delicate path you will walk. Emotions may resurge and tempt the *Detachment in Love* traveler to allow a relapse into a former consciousness of Attachment with its pitfalls ... whence this transmutation Process will need repeating <u>until you're anchor is set!</u>
Be most self-observant in these times, Dear Ones, caring tenderly with Self-Love for your Process, as you savor the joy and newly gained Freedom along the way.

Last and not least, let Me enhance your vibration of Detachment to include My gift of Love without strings. *'Letting go' with Love intact is a beauteous route to include in your Relationship journey. Once Detached, ongoing contact, less the physical aspects of passionate attraction if that be, can oft be beautifully maintained to the betterment of All. And, of course, sometimes not!.*

On your Earth plane ... this change in your state of mind is sometimes known as 'parting as best of friends'. Can you perceive the Win-Win solution peeking its head into the mix here?

Holding lightly, without clinging, your connections with people, things, and beliefs ... will ironically reward you in quality of life, believe Me! And know *there is space* in there for your intentions, passions, and focus of forward motion toward your free-will objectives!

So, Detachment with Love, in action, beyond a mere conceptual understanding, brings your consciousness into a heightened vibration, leaving behind the former blockages of your evolution, barriers that otherwise would restrict and impede you if a captive.

Similar to shifting *Judgment into Non-Judgment*, shifting *Attachments* is equally impactive when translated into *Detachments with Love*.

Conquer these two ways of Being, and other milestones of Mastery yet to be revealed to you, and you will be blessed and amazed at your progress walking in the Light.

Yes, I know, change may be contrary to the comfort of your particular Human condition which seeks permanence. And yet with responsible Detachment, the above change in your approach to living will expand your consciousness into new vistas upon horizons yet to be newly perceived.

Step up and step out! Live life fully engaged yet unattached to the outcome of every moment. Your best moments may be temporary as well as seemingly enduring. Savor your blessings, you deserve them!

Mark My words as you travel through your process, and you will have some amusing ah ha moments to share with Me!

Keep a watchful eye upon your Grand Process, Folks! Balance in relationship is supported by clear perspectives *that embody alignment for the ultimate good of the Soul(s) that are connected to their Grand Process.*

The *centerpiece* image, in perspective, that I described earlier needs be held clearly in mind throughout the course of a relationship, *and yet, ironically, not to dilute the passion and Love that can inspire, nourish and grow without hindering!* Notice My words about 'bonding without binding' as you read on.

And Yes, indeed, We recognize this is asking a considerable stretch of your consciousness, as your priorities may seem to conflict at first, until you acclimatize. Are you now a *Friend of Change*?

Now for the Romantics. For those who view themselves as incurable romantics, … this Wisdom may be a difficult pill to swallow. How can such an inclusive simultaneous loyalty … shared between Self, We, and Spirit … be possible, you would ask?

As you escape the clutches of your Attachments, opening the door to expand these loyalties to My Wisdom, All will magically realign to be included in your Grand Process. *A stretch of your consciousness will suffice, be it altogether or in stages.*

And, recall that your free-will still has veto power to insist that Ego reign supreme at the exclusion of Spirit. The Karmic wheel has many vacant seats for those who wish to make their reservation as they *go it alone.* *Countless seats are filled* **with dedicated Ego champions of the 3rd Dimension.**

On the contrary, Mastery of the 'We and Me Perspective' holds you in the Light, acknowledging the Human urges of Oneness within you.

And then there is another polar opposite extreme. For those not *yet open to including Spirit's Wisdom in their life-stream, this is your free-will choice as well. All things in their good time! And for those who* possess the self-absorbed Ego-dominated traits of Narcissism, … know that these behaviors encapsulate Ego Attachment and Addiction in the highest degree! *The Narcissist's reality believes that Ego is the centerpiece, and there is therefore no difficult 'We' pill to swallow!*

It is all about them, and there is no 'We'. Deeply imbedded, although often cleverly disguised, this is a prime motivation in <u>Ego's use</u> of free-will that holds captive as the Narcissist. Now you know!

This Ego-dominant style, absent to One's own Higher-Self, *is often forcefully imposed* up*on a partner.* Balance remains absent, and Spirit has no opportunity to bless the Narcissist, inextricably stubborn, Ego-bound and self-serving. Ones holding this extreme Self-image as dominant in their consciousness, ... actually believe this illusion is always justifiable, and fight for their entitlement! These Ones are ***fully oblivious to the gigantic illusion holding them captive!*** Oblivious to consequences, such Ones are often unhappy on the Earth plane, and end up upon the Karmic wheel holding their same reserved seat!

೭೦⋘

What about Bonding? Can bonding occur without Binding Attachment? *Again, ... yes, of course, provided that bonding carries the coefficient of Freedom as I have stated numerous times in this transmission!* Listen carefully here ...the answer can thereby be <u>*yes or no*</u> depending upon the <u>level of My Wisdom that is Mastered by you and your partner(s)</u>. *Re-read this a few times, Dear Ones, before your eyes move on!*

Mastery brings happiness that flows in to
the mix
like honey from the hive you have created!

☙❧

When you hold **Love and Joy,** *without possessiveness, dependency nor fear of loss, you are approaching the vibration of Mastery* in Relationship that sheds those colors of disappointment, ... and places Detachment with Love in your proper aligned perspective.

Once a delicate perspective of balance is achieved
in some degree of Mastery,
happiness flows in to the mixture
like honey from the hive you have created!

☙❧

Love shows us life in different colours.

Yes, ... *The Magic of Oneness* prevails again, Oneness with your Relationship, and ironically, still allowing space for your thriving Personal Universe held in the arms of Spirit. You may have discovered that I, as Saint Germain, support Win-Win solutions in harmony.

These Perspectives about 'We and Me' are prime examples of such a Divine construction.
We have gone full circle.

Enjoy the journey, My Dear Ones. Seek and  find the Light with your partners, and thou shalt be the benefactor of joy and happiness along the way. May peace and harmony

Bless you Always.

I bid you good Day.

Saint Germain

and Lah Rahn Ananda aka Gordon Corwin II

Chapter 14

Adulthood
And Family Relationship

As a young person grows into maturity and **prepares to leave the nest**, with new wings poised to fly, *the inevitable* will surface: 'whether or not I will start living my new life engulfed, shackled and dominated by my family's beliefs and traditional status quo values, … or will I follow my heart and its calling, with my own passion, to live a violet life of merit as I choose, … a life without judgmental limitation or enforced family tradition?'

This is a primary question and choice for a young adult. And sometimes, this very issue lingers on into later life of an *older* adult, confused about making wise choices of whether to follow their own dharma or to live a life duplicating the dharma of another. Does this ring a bell with you?

Notice, My Dear Ones, how Humanity has been historically plagued for centuries of Earth time, drenched in outdated, generational family consciousness patterns. These are often cultural, with pressing demands for upcoming generations to follow and to be bound by the beliefs, behaviors, and *choices of family elders. Man's recorded collective history will show these traits and choices largely to be the very causes of non-evolvement, status quo stagnation, and collective stagnation among Humans.* Observe the non-evolvement in overall collective and individual Human behavior over the centuries and the resulting *chaotic outcome in your World drenched in your non-evolution today during your so called modern times!*

A young person's *fundamental family relationship choice* at the outset of Adulthood is to decide whether or not to accept parts, or perhaps none, of the traditional 'family consciousness' as a guideline for their upcoming life, albeit many such traditions of consciousness are sadly frozen solid in

time, stuck by elder mandate! Blind acceptance, without question runs the risk of a lifetime repeating old patterns that have not stood the *test of time* nor allowed for evolvement of consciousness.

When a young person's life-choices are self-forfeited, a new life-stream of promise *risks* being convoluted by carrying 'old family ways', biases, judgments, beliefs and behaviors that otherwise could be *freely chosen to transcend … into an extraordinary realm, … empowering a young rising person of potential to drink from a full cup of life resting alongside Universal Law.*

Stated another way, if I may be blunt, … journeying into Adulthood poses a question: 'Am I going to live my life to please my parent(s) … or will I now choose to follow *my own inner voice* of passion to live, …with *my own* choices and perceptions, … in harmony with every living thing?' Ponder this!

Now here is a Soul request that may stretch your consciousness to comply. Will you claim your right to *Freedom of responsible choices* in your own life, *and yet embrace, in balance and perspective, your Love of family and fellow man?*

Behold Human history! Carte Blanche *acceptance of unenlightened influences of the ages*, with *a clear recorded history of separation and incorrigible, stubborn Egos at work*, … carries this gigantic price. This status quo of consciousness over centuries, though not without occasional merit, has nonetheless led Humanity's collective behavior to demonstrate itself to be clearly counter to choices of higher calling … to walk aligned paths into the Light with Love, ease and grace!

So now, We can mine the gold together in Relationship! As young Ones, with these Truths now in hand, *you All have license of Human free-will to choose Freedom as a guiding Light embedded with Love, Oneness, Integrity, and aligned Worldly actions for the Highest Good! You will be Lovingly embraced by Me and the Ascended Realm Above as you take this described Joyful Journey of Choice, My Dear Friends.*

In the Light,

Saint Germain

Through Lah Rahn Ananda aka Gordon Corwin II 06-03-2019

Chapter 15

ATTACHMENT

'Attachment is the source of all Suffering.'
Buddha

The Big Picture? You <u>or</u> the other person(s) may be feeling that this relationship has played itself out? Or perhaps it no longer serves the *mutual or personal purpose(s)* intended in the beginning? Or the flame of passion has dwindled and an ongoing friendship not kindled? ... Or that you yourself believe you have now learned the intended life's lessons? ... Or that you <u>or</u> your partner are simply quitting, giving up! *Or that you* would like to *remain* partnered and

have the Freedom to grow together and be bonded without the burdens and pains of Attachment? So many conditions and feelings.

We in Spirit, along with your Soul-self can coach you to: *diligently mine the gold from the life's lessons offered, heed the teachings, integrate them into your life in the now, and gracefully be in Relationship, ... or to move on having Detached with Love as your choice would have it.*

Before making your choices, consult with us, if you would like, about the <u>extent of your completion of the life's lessons</u> in this relationship. Is it 100% and free-flowing, or 85%, or maybe just 50 %, at this time? We will guide you in *your choices*, and concurrently, *know that We will not make them for you,* as part of this process is for your consciousness and Soul-self to decide upon. *We do not override or violate the Human gift of Free-will that blesses all Humanity in their Earthly incarnations, even as Attachment may nonetheless take its toll as a life's lesson runs its course.*

This Chapter 'Attachment' is meant to address some of the general, common, bare threads that appear to Us, Ascended Above, as challenges and break-ups show their faces throughout Human behaviors.

As We have discussed earlier, CHANGE is a *certainty* **surrounding Human Life. All relationships have no immunity to change, though they may carry the** *intention* **lasting for a lifetime! Could this irony be a surprise to you? Remember this old adage: in Human life events you can usually observe** *a beginning, a middle, and an end. The 'when' becomes the question.*

So now, comes the moment of choice and hopefully the moment of Truth! Continuing or Moving On from a relationship brings out the price of Attachment, often a real speed bump in the road, sometimes a shattering event. Expect that some conscious processing and growth on your part is needed to reach closure and conclusion for your choices. Hopefully, it will extend to healing and closure, whatever the outcome, for others involved as well.

The amount and intensity varies greatly with each individual, depending upon the depth of relationship, Karma involved, Soul mate history and life's lessons in this incarnation. Renewed promises or a break may be orchestrated with friendliness, ease and grace, **or** be it heated and spiced with angst, unlearned lessons to be repeated, or with convoluted disparities, grudges, lack of forgiveness, and whatever else untamed Egos would contribute.

Divine prescriptions and insights are offered to lead you through the healing process, blending ingredients to include awareness, change, ease and grace, forgiveness, Self- love, clear communication, and compassion, and patience. Do you notice the similarity between these foregoing elements and those We started in coaching you with initially forming and maintaining a Relationship? Yes Folks, there are *common denominators to consider at this juncture* ... starting at the beginning, continuing in the middle, and at the end: Union, Attachment, Detachment with Love, and Moving On!

Also, as I have stated earlier, there is a great overlap of many entwined relationship issues and grey areas addressed in this book. I remind you that there is much to be gained **through repetition, re-reading and review** in the learning process … and this book is no exception. Also, you will notice intentional repetitions for your edification and enlightenment.

Objectives?

In any case, ideal objectives, as you deal with the realities of Attachment, (as well as of Detachment, and Moving On), would *include* peaceful resolutions, completions filled with gratitude for the life's lessons given and hopefully learned. Wisely appreciate the joys in the process along the journey, with pleasant and positive memories that mark meaningful times together thus far.

The catch here is to be able to recognize your life's lessons from this relationship, and then … *to apply the lessons to your new thinking and elevated behavior patterns with higher vibrations than before you began*.

Throughout this transmutation process, **open communication**, of course, opens the door for authenticity and a much deeper meaning to relationship experience, long or short. Open and honest communication at this juncture will enrich your experience, and yet, often We observe that Egos stick belligerently to their beliefs and stories that caused the ruckus or the breakup, *without being vulnerable to honestly share the part that their OWN Ego's* *sang in this chorus ... mostly off-key notes, sung with conviction and self-righteous indignation!*

This inauthentic and armor-shielded Ego behavior *cheats you out of the life's lessons, Folks, ... the very gifts that your relationship has brought unto you for the taking!*

Tender yourself in the arms of Self-love as you seek out memories of those relationship experiences that bring or have brought joy to you and /or your partner. Seek and embrace your shared love, the life's lessons learned, and Win-Win outcomes that you created together as 'Us'.

Nota Bene. *Egos dream in vain* that they are clever enough to fool your Soul-self and Spirit too, while <u>Karma prevails and continues to repeat the life's lesson that you may be missing altogether!</u> Sound familiar? Have you noticed, they do repeat? Have you brought change to your way of Being to make needed alterations to Karmic patterns?

Here Is An Offer from Spirit ...
Hard to Refuse?

We offer you Our Divine energies and coaching which can bring you great relief from *imagined or real burdens.*

In your quiet personal moments communing with Spirit in direct contact with Us, you may choose to 'give back to Spirit' ... *once you have done your one hundred % best to conquer your unsolved Attachment issues, those challenges that are seemingly stuck and won't budge!*

Simply ask Ourselves to take these *specific* **issues from you.** We gratefully assist many of you in this way and hear your gratefulness as you speak it to Us, directly or in prayer.

Notice the great relief, *perhaps with a <u>sigh of newly found Freedom</u>, when you fully engage with Us in doing this transformative process with Our support!*

Let the Light come in to surround and dissipate the darkness of unresolved negative attachments you may

have. **Breakups have no shortages of negativity!** The time would be now to choose a higher vibration pattern, and resist any temptation to sink down into lower levels chosen by others, as some breakup behaviors We observe from Above. This higher vibrational choice precludes 'tit for tat' behavior, a long time favorite of hemorrhaging Egos!

Freedom is priceless, Folks. If there is ever a time for positive indulgence, this is it ... indulge yourself in the Light leading into your new dimension of Freedom.

As Lord Saint Germain, I invite you to be My guest in My Crystal Cave of Light, on behalf of the Entire Ascended Realm. I await your call.

When 110% of YOUR part of the work is done, you are especially deserving of our services. We are most receptive to aligned requests, when you have truly exhausted *your own resources, and the rest is perhaps beyond Human reach.* (Tell the truth, We are watching).

As you see, We can fill in many pieces of your consciousness that you are unable to access, leading you to newly found Freedoms, ... as you move through Attachment, Detachment, and MOVE ON, if that be your choice. Many of you Chelas and Spirit seekers of Light can bear witness to our powers to absorb and dissolve negative energies.

Taking it all so personally? Remember that when you are impacted by others' harsh behavior, often it has originated and stemmed from deep and visceral chasms within the other's consciousness, perhaps from early childhood, or from taught ancestral behaviors. And, at a particular moment, this behavior may be <u>'venting loudly'</u> and seemingly *directed straight at you!* And yet, it is just the way other Ones are wired and constructed! Before you even came along into the picture!

Thus, ... it can seem to be so very personal. It may not be. And, of course, Noblesse Oblige can nicely enter the big picture, if warranted by your situation and choice.

A venting person can be automatically acting out a default behavior, one that they are not conscious of in that moment. Hopefully, you have learned to recognize such past patterns in a partner before they cause you undue angst, sleepless nights, or reach inflammatory proportions that could move On stage.

Also, remember that a behavior coming straight at you *can carry an energy seemingly venomous to you.* <u>And yet, the dispensing actor is often oblivious to the effect their behavior has on others</u> ... and sometimes does not have the intention of deep injury or hurtfulness. Perhaps it's just the way they are Being at this point in their life process? Here an illusion on your part can prevent you from gaining higher ground unless you see through it.

Let Us now speak about how your Attachments can be so forcefully interwound with the Freedom process.

What can you do to set yourself free? So now, here comes the *real potential challenge for many*:

This would be dealing with Attachment! It is part and parcel of the 'Staying in' phase *and/or* the 'Moving On' phase. For clarity We speak now about first of the three parts of letting go.

Surely, the degree of your Attachment to a relationship *will dictate intensity of many emotions (and perhaps obsession with drama) that would appear to you, passive or vivid! Your emotions can be signposts and gifts telling you of issues to which you can isolate, give your conscious attention, and now Master! This will take commitment, and you will need to dig deeply into your own personal Universe to have <u>resolutions of Truth that will stay with you for this lifetime, without relapse.</u>*

An <u>Ongoing</u> Attachment is a *Stuckness* pattern that sometimes adheres during this process, where often a partner can be unaware of their particular behavior patterns until they bring awareness of stuckness to the surface. *Know that Egos can source stuckness. <u>Egos can ignite a part of you that is more satisfied to be stuck than to move on from Attachment! Beware of this potential trap that asks for your incarceration!</u> If wise, you will re-read this paragraph!*

It (the pattern) can be broken by aware insightful self-correction, with absolute honesty and discipline, devoid of excuses, and introduction of new horizons to cloud the issue at hand!

To expand your resources of recognizing Attachment as it clings to you, consider the *habitual* *default thinking patterns* that you have developed regarding a relationship.

If Moving On is in your picture, this is the plural orientation, <u>often the admirable 'We' and 'Us' pattern and mind set, may need to be altered now to move away from this default thinking pattern that many have formerly so much needed.</u> The plural can become so routine, and deeply ingrained into your consciousness, … that it now keeps you from moving on. Yes? Are we speaking about CHANGE and new realities that need to be accommodated?

Some Clarity at this point. Unyielding Attachment is often confused with Unwavering commitment, loyalty and dedication!

T**he key insight here is to focus upon the intent: If the choice is to release Attachment, let those feelings be revealed.** **The Buddha has much to say in this regard.** He points out that Attachment is a primary cause of suffering. Have you noticed that you can become Attached to suffering at times? Have you honestly noticed? Take a moment to make a note of some Attachment examples in your life?

_____
_____
_____

_____
_____
_____
_____
_____
_____
_____
_____

ఇంచి

So then, you ask how can I be 'successful' in the 3rd dimensional World without being *Attached*?   Or, to put it another way, how can I be 'successful' in attaining goals … if I Am *detached, (erroneously interpreted as <u>uncommitted</u>)* as I go about other important parts of my life?

To paraphrase Myself, the secret of Mastering Attachment lies in *the aligned <u>energy you shift to the Detachment with Love Process</u>* **with integrity and surrender yet with uncompromised intention!**

Also concurrently, the secret lies in the energy you divert from the Outcome not <u>meeting your expectations or demands</u> to <u>surrendering willingly to 'what is' in these moments.</u>   Acceptance?

Giving your 110% personal best effort, … *with the stark reality in mind that 'after my best effort, the outcome will be what it will be'… this allows you a clear and* *positive intention and dedication to allowing the outcome to Be in your own consciousness!*

Ironically enough, an enlightened Detachment to the outcome <u>minimizes or eliminates the often upsetting impact of Attachments to unfulfilled expectations, while clearing the way for possibility.</u>

Liken all of this to rolling with the punch, and taking it in stride! *And then 'getting over it'.* Acceptance and Forgiveness will transport you to new heights during your release process here. We suggest this as a daily routine in your Moving On daily disciplines and routines. *Note:* **Forgiveness and Compassion are so very important that We give space <u>in its own separate Chapter of this book</u>.**

*** And consider this: Attachment is very easily confused with qualities of *clear intention, dedication and devotion.* **Meditate upon this until you are clear, Dear Friends! A clear and quiet mind can easily distinguish.**

Ones can be Attached to many things: to Attachment itself, to suffering, to 'success', to the outcome, to self-sabotage, to being famous, to being the victim, money, sexual expressions, and yes, even to being loved, etc. etc. Which of these or others may apply to you in your experiences so far?

*Check them off **in your case, and tell the truth to yourself**!*

- ☐ Attachment to Fear
- ☐ Attachment to Resisting Change
- ☐ Attachment to Keeping a Relationship
- ☐ Attachment to Suffering
- ☐ Attachment to Your *Investment*
- ☐ Attachment to Your Illusion
- ☐ Attachment to My Right of Entitlement
- ☐ Attachment to being Impatient
- ☐ Attachment to being Right
- ☐ Attachment to being Loved
- ☐ Attachment to the Person (s) involved
- ☐ Attachment to your Emotion(s)
- ☐ Attachment to Dominating Others
- ☐ Attachment to Anger
- ☐ Attachment to not being Judged by …..
- ☐ Attachment to Discarding it all! Quitting!
- ☐ Attachment to Having it Your Way!
- ☐ Attachment to Your Default Behaviors
- ☐ Attachment to Money

Make your Personal List:

_____

_____

※※

At this point, also be aware of *the difference between your ATTACHMENT to the Relationship itself or to your INVESTMENT in the Relationship.*

Naturally a sincere, motivated, enlivened and dedicated relationship partner can make humongous *investments* of energy, time, ideas, work, love, good faith, heartful energies … all aimed at relationship success.

Without these sorts of investments, the relationship vibration may stall out early on, as you may have experienced.

Half-assed approaches to relationship rarely bear the fruit. The tree is starved because the roots lack nourishment to thrive! Your *Investment* is part of the game and it may be *at risk, a known risk <u>at the start if you are aware!</u>* Did you expect absolute guarantees in life?

There are benefits to *going 'all in'* with your very best efforts, wrapped in the *intention of success* and achieving the intended outcomes. With this said, however, periodic monitoring of certain benchmark milestones, evaluating the situation, and *making changes to the intensity of your 'giving of self' is a wise practice*, ... for all partners, separately and collectively.

Now that you have a greater understanding of Attachments and related parts, let Us turn to the next phase, the middle phase, I shall call

'Detachment with Love'.

Blessings and My most heartful compassion as you move through this process. Heart-wrenching at times, as it may be, you are empowered to go through and move on with this journey of Practical Spirituality. You are commended for your courage, Dear Friends!

With love and compassion
in the Light,

Saint Germain
and the Realm

Through Lah Rahn Ananda aka Gordon Corwin II

Chapter 16

Detaching from a Loved One

A Personal Experience of the Author

About one hour before my Loved One's conscious transition into the arms of God, this beautiful Being came to me with parting words of wisdom. Her words were sourced from the Angelic Kingdom, from which her lifetime was cast, I later discovered. Her voice was clear, silent and calm. Her wisdom was lovingly intended to prepare me for her transition, starting that moment and to then complete in one more hour. Knowing that her transition would be a massively heart-wrenching change in my life, and that I would need her advice, she kindly sent words of Wisdom in those parting moments. Her transmission was loving and soft, simply saying to me:

"Remember to celebrate all those many wonderful years and joyful times that we have had together".

"Love me deeply, but do not love me too much".

These words were her last. And with her last breath, she closed her eyes for the last time.

After some months of contemplation and emotional adjustment to this profound change in my life, *I realized she was advising me about creating my own <u>bridge into Detachment with Love</u>, and learning to move along with ease and grace, beyond an understandable grieving period. And then to further learn about moving beyond pain and suffering that a lingering <u>Attachment could otherwise bring,</u> if chosen to allow.*

This was about 9 years ago. Since then, I have gratefully used this advice on many occasions to bring ease and grace to my own process of *appropriate Detaching with Love*, as these choices inevitably pop up in my life-stream. As much as ever, I Am still reminded that Her supportive advice, wrapped in aligned reality, has served me well. *I hope you will allow this blessing to serve you as well.*

I invite you to intake this gift of Detachment advice, as did I, in a Spirit of Self-love, and that you may also fulfill your relationship completions in *Mastering Detachment with Love* in place of holding on to Attachment with suffering. This was a big lesson for me. I Am truly grateful to have had this healing life experience delivered by Spirit at just the right time. As always, Spirit's advice of Wisdom continues to serve me in extraordinary ways with deep and profound effects. I pray that you will also benefit from this account of my heartful journey of *Detachment with Love*, and that Light will shine upon you along your path ahead.

May you be Blessed always.

    Love,

       Jah Rahn

Chapter 17

Detachment
Walking the Fine Line

At the outset, We say that 'Oneness' is a basic element in the structure of Divine consciousness. As aspirants of this Ascended level of consciousness, you, My Dear Ones, are wise to bear Oneness in mind ... as We speak now of Detachment. At the end of this incarnation and in transition, you will realize that We are all One, indeed.

And, the irony here is that throughout a Human lifetime there is a Spiritual part of you that is a part of the *All of All Oneness ... and at the same time,* in order to evolve, *there are times when you must create space for the individual growth of your part in* *relationships. Consider your boundaries, as you use and direct your energies toward that from which you are detaching.*

My first question to you. Are you willing to stop feeding energy to that from which you want to detach? Careful here, this becomes tricky!

So, We speak here not of a separation between Beings, where Love could fade away, but of placing an appropriate distance or 'space' between relationship partners, such that each partner can lovingly Move On to allow evolution of their own Soul path, and of their partner(s).

Surely you know by now that relationship partners commonly evolve at different speeds and at different times. When a partnership of once mutually shared paths takes a diversion of direction, a fork in the road, *you may come to the point of choosing Detachment, ... and in the former context, please! That would be 'Detachment with Love'.*

On a lower 3rd dimensional level, Ones in their Detaching process often metaphorically ask Us about their relationship '<u>when</u> do I stop beating a dead horse?' In response, they often hear 'when you get sick and tired of being sick and tired of that', and when your free-will steps in with a choice. This may be at a point of full <u>depletion of the willingness to continue or at a point where there is more patience required than either you or a partner(s) are capable of, ... or willing ... to bring to the table</u>. Or perhaps a reorganization of energies is needed to smooth out some speed bumps and restart anew? <u>Your choice</u>. <u>And their choice.</u>

I hasten to also mention the role of Forgiveness in the Detachment process. *Forgiveness of self and others is an often overlooked gateway to moving on beyond a speed bump or onto Detachment. I refer to responsibly jettisoning past actions, outcomes and circumstances that could hold you captive.* A formal Forgiving process, with you as the Forgiver, is recommended.

Perhaps this process is done by yourself. Or, perhaps a mentor or trusted colleague can assist you to cover all the bases, to forgive what is to be forgiven, and to thereby allow yourself to move on with Detachment with Love and to Freedom.

ॐ

Detachment and Change

During a devoted partnership transition (and the relationship Detachment that goes hand in hand), be aware of a mentality that habitually thinks 'We and Us', when in fact, <u>there is often no more we and us in a literal sense. And still, We and Us and I are connected as part of the All.</u> This irony must be remembered as you proceed.

A plural 'We' orientation was set up in the beginning as a foundation that you could then build upon. Remember the previous Chapters referred to a structure of Us and We as desirable to set up early on in the relationship? And, of course, it was done piece by piece, at the propitious moments, to add some groundwork for relationship harmony, team work and stability building.

Well, here you are facing Change, ... now beginning to *dismantle certain structures of a relationship, if it no longer works to serve the highest good.* The key point of focus is how you go about this, and about wrapping your emotions and actions, *still engaged in Love,* inside of your Process!

And yes, there are limbo exceptions to modifying the Us, possibly where children are involved, elder parents, and many more variations of Us'. Sometimes, the plural *continues on and on over time.* Do you recall Chapter 14 "Adulthood"?

As We and Us, there are *naturally ingrained habits of previous choice, and* these can now present a challenge of change. That was then, and this is now. Remember my words about impermanence of Human life? <u>**Now, when things have changed**, *these habits may persist and cause suffering from Attachment, if you are not careful.***</u>

During this letting go process, when present reality says something is over for you, *a feeling of emptiness inside can understandably appear, nagging with a temptation to revert back to the habitual default behavior and thinking patterns I have just mentioned.*

Change, unless you have cultivated its friendship, presents challenges to many. Detachment is no exception. The temptation here is to linger, retelling your small Detachment story and anxieties to yourself ... (or others) ... **over and over and over again, ad nauseum, until this ego pattern itself becomes your default, a new captivating and negative habit, in and of itself! Surely you recognize this reactivation in full motion?**

Certainly, the Ego receives its payoff in such cases. It *reinforces its position of being right, bolstering pseudo self–esteem, being separate from higher vibrations of Spirit and your true self, and of <u>staying stuck</u> in the status quo that needs updating! Are you with Me? Need to re-read? It is understandable, this is meaty mentoring!*

After a breakup, be sure not to let this re-telling of the small story extend beyond a 30-day habit forming period, as this behavior can then become 'stuck' and you sink deeper into the quagmire! *Let staying centered be one of your guidelines, Folks. Regular meditation is highly recommended. We are headed together here toward a goal of evolvement, Love and Freedom for All relationship partners involved.*

Was there one relationship partner who wanted to continue and one that wanted to break up? Just beware you *may need to manage an emotion of abandonment, which can creep in for the partner wanting to hang on.* Could this be you? *If so, your Detachment process needs to acknowledge this emotion and add in healing energies to transcend residual distress that may linger on.* **Remember, Moving On is next!**

Reactivation
A Habit of Choice

Now, at this juncture, it is so tempting to re-tell the *highly triggering stories of past incidents, either by self-talk or actual conversations with those who will listen.*

These re-tellings can also become a Habit, <u>where triggering incidents of the relationship are repeated, on and on</u>, to self and/or others for days, months, and sometimes even years, in perpetuity *UNTIL you break the cycle or you don't!* Completion is often the missing link to break the cycle.

**MOVE ON WITH EASE and GRACE!
SEEK COMPLETION!
GET OVER IT!**

Human lifetime experiences are all part of the Journey with no guarantees.

**Do your best to take outcomes in stride.
Drink the nectar from your life's lessons with love.**

Forgiveness and prayer are keys to release you from the reactivation grip, to assist you in forming new habit patterns of completion as replacements vs. continuing behavior *solidifying a re-attachment cycle.*

Recurring Re-activation episodes, especially where you believe (justly or in your Illusion) that you were hurt, injured emotionally or physically, treated unfairly, used, betrayed, etc. … need be recognized for what they are and addressed in a timely way. Here again, Self-love has it's opportunity to come forward, to stand and be counted! *(see preceding Chapter 7 'Discovering Your Triggers'). Allowing indulgence in re-activation episodes to continue* will then undoubtedly cause continued suffering, and prolonged attachment even long after a breakup has occurred! These episodes can manifest as sleepless nights, renewed anger, bitterness, obsessions, health problems, and ultimately affect the quality of your life. **Detachment moves you forward where re-activation episodes can then dissipate!**

I**t is good to be extremely conscious about this 'thing' called Reactivation**, especially at this point in your relationship journey.

Reactivation is a recalling and reenactment, *a very vivid and re-created state of emotion, where you actually relive specific past incidents in your present moments! (Although you are present only in your mind, you have vividly reverted and re-created the past.* Reactivation episodes are *where your Ego compulsively re-creates and falls back into the same emotional state you were mightily engaged in when it really happened!* You have lapsed back in time, to repeat the episode, vividly reliving former states of elation, pleasure, agitation, anger, suffering, distress, etc. that was there earlier when it happened. Note: negatives are more easily reactivated than positives ... and yes, there are exceptions, I joyfully add!

Episodes, as I say, can be positive or negative. *Positives include wonderful memories of good times, heartful interchanges, tears of joy, pleasures, synchronicities, gifts of great personal importance, and other things received joyfully with gratitude, Love, and enthusiasm, bringing you happiness.*

Negatives are the tricky part. The context here is where you relive the past *issues that perhaps triggered you <u>and are not yet complete</u>,* or have left some unhealed emotional scar, real or imagined.

Mentally reenacting negative episode(s), in a move to re-nforce your position or memories in the

earlier experience, can often justify the illusion of your Ego behavior, being 'right' and *continuing to make wrong what distressed you, from your perspective at that past point in time!* This is especially true with negative reactivations.

*** In a reactivation illusion of being in present time, often old incomplete or broken communications in the orignial breakdown are imagined to be in the present, now being spoken after the fact, *often to one's self and/or to others as your small* story. During reactivation episodes, that thinking somehow believes that history can be re-written, and the eggs can be re-scrambled.

As you work to break the cycle, gaining balanced Detachment with Love will require your aware discipline, concentration, and focus, Dear Friends. Attention to avoid reverting to old reactivation habit patterns is crucial to your future of **Moving On,** … a subject to follow!

Bonded or Bound

Let it be said that We are all bonded together as One in the grandest sense, albeit Beings now in Ascended Spirit, or you now incarnated in Human flesh. This greater connection embraces an all

*encompassing visceral flow of shared energy ...
We Above refer to this Truth as Oneness.*

In your relationship(s) you may appreciate this greater connection, regardless of the personal Ego dynamics in play. Be it a relationship in the formation building stage, the middle or the end phases, **always remember your Universal heritage of relationship to All living things.**

When Bonding is intensified into a tightly held, forever-binding Attachment ... never ever to escape your clutch and grasp, ... know that you are Bound and obsessed!

That said, as We now address Detachment, there are particulars that must be realized and addressed, in order for you to arrive at completion and the peace and Freedom I champion.

The task at hand, aside from being *appropriately* Bonded as I have indicated, may involve further actions on your part ... an *Unbinding* from those Attachments that are no longer wanted or needed. **Your list has its own unique issues.**

Your task is to create this list below and follow through. Graceful Detachment embodies heartful caring and heartful sharing, *held loosely as Freedom replaces the Attachments at issue.*

Resistance to the Process, We have seen from Above, is often a favorite tool of Ego that holds Illusion to be sacred at all costs. *Unfortunately for you, this cost you shall bear until change says otherwise.*

Do these words ring a bell for you? An Ego justifying resistance often says: 'I'm upset and for good reason! I get satisfaction from being upset and I want to stay that way!' 'I know I am always right!' 'I'm pissed and I will stay that way!' (Upset is prolonged and reinforced until the illusion becomes reality?)

Have you ever examined the payoff your Ego gets by <u>staying in the upset</u>. The payoff boils down to : 'I'm right! He, She, it was/is wrong', *and sometimes 'I'm addicted to pain and I like it!'*

Telling yourself the Truth (beyond the self-lies and imaginary comforts found inside your Ego's nest) can do wonders in accelerating your progress to release Attachments and Ego illusions in favor of reality and thence elevate into the Freedoms you seek.

While the Duality on your Earth fosters energies of opposites, dark and light, positive and negative, etc., ... Illusion even further clouds the Duality, by holding sacred and *superimposed, <u>man-made judgments of 'right and wrong'</u>*. Reality in Spirit holds no right or wrong, only what is and what is not.

Relationship Illusion

As you play your role on the stage of Human relationship, be keenly aware, observing that Illusion commonly walks into center position. When the Truth of a relationship (to yourself and to others alike) is clearly seen, the illusion miraculously fades into Reality. *'I'm shocked! The relationship partner is not who I thought they were and/or would be'.* Does this sound familiar?

Reality says illusionary hopes and dreams unfulfilled can cause upset, pain and suffering if you remain attached to the illusion. When you transform into a full awareness of Detachment, a magical spell of peace and tranquility will overtake, as a breath of fresh air, as a soothing of your skin and a pleasant brushing through your hair. You are now standing in the rewarding space of Truth!

This conscious change gives a wondrous new space to your Being. Your outlook and expectations are given wiggle room to *evolve past the illusion* as they will, to morph into higher vibrations. You will know when this process prevails and Attachment with Suffering fades into the dusk in favor of Detachment with Love!

The Tradeoff

In a simple phrase, this conscious tradeoff is your choice. The energy you could invest in your Attachment is exchanged for rewards of energy <u>newly directed to *Detachment with Love*</u>. The out of balance becomes in balance. Your upsets, frustrations, dashed hopes and dreams, are traded for peace, knowing that *'the what is' … is O.K. with you and now viewed as a type of Love'*.

New Freedoms, now at hand, come to the fore, with new paths and open space for you to BE in the now. Go there!

Ghosting
Walking Out

When the going gets tough, certain partner(s) in relationship can choose to simply walk out! This is sometimes referred to as 'Ghosting', in your Gen X and Y slang terms. Earlier, it was called 'Shining' someone, in your Worldly lingo.

I mention this here, as such behavior is becoming more prevalent in Gen –X, Y and Internet dating circles, although it is not new to older generations, just less prevalent or visible. Be aware that Ghosting is passive-aggressive behavior.

Clearly, a person(s) who chooses to ghost someone else is abruptly bailing out of this relationship, without notice! And without further communication! We observe that this *disappearing act* can be permanent or temporary, depending upon levels of caring, future change(s) of heart or attitude.

When communications continue to be disrupted or cut off, We *clearly see from Above that the whole relationship status is seriously disrupted if not essentially terminated.* Endings of this sort sadly lack the open connections to, at a minimum, bringing about a peaceful and harmonious wind-up and completions. Chaos stemming from emotional states can easily enter the picture now. **Can you see how Spiritual alignment is blatantly absent when ghosting is practiced? Remember, Order is the First Law of the Divine!**

Why do people Ghost?
Irresponsibly Avoiding their own integrity and emotional discomfort are the primary reasons. There is no positive consideration for the feelings of the other person in such cases, only the 'I'. Ghosts show they would rather simply walk out, *even if there are social consequences, or self- emotional consequences of shame or guilt! The cost can be high!! If you are Soul mates, now or in former lifetimes, there can be Karmic consequences, causing <u>repeat</u> life-lesson requirements to newly lay ahead.*

The sad reality here is *that the more often Ghosters do it,* or have it <u>done to them</u> *by relationship partners, the more desensitized and calloused they become to this type of behavior, and the more common it becomes. Does this make it acceptable? Self-love along with outward Love, decency and respect of your brothers and sisters would say NO, of course not.*

You are all here to learn to Love each other (in different ways, of course, and <u>relationships are among the highest and best life lesson teachers of all time!</u>

People who Ghost have their many justifications:

I got mad and *could not face* my own emotions.

Too much trouble to talk it out and rebalance.

I just do not care.

I don't have the courage.

Relationship integrity is not a priority for me.

Said yes when I should have said no.

I get *annoyed* when I have to clean up a relationship situation.

I am *impatient* about relationship conversations.

I *don't know* how to handle confrontation.

I'm afraid I will *lose my power if I am vulnerable* to talk it out.

I may *risk exposing new parts of my true self,* etc.

In some ways We see that the practice of positive **relationship dynamics is truly an art!** Learned skill, with heart level engagement, comes easily for some, and is a challenge for others who find *unresolved relationship issues* showing up regularly in their lives, over and over again, same patterns. much like one of your broken LP over, and with the repeating Very playing old records!

> *Milking out the very last drops of life lessons, and making the decisive higher vibrational Changes in behavior ... can break stagnant cycles, opening space for a real Freedom that refreshes the Soul with Freedom!*

Conscious Thoughts and Actions

Holding yourself **Attached and Bound** inside of a relationship will further *prolong your transition to Detachment with Love.* Many of you hold habitual, *sometimes obsessive-compulsive, patterns of habits* that keep you locked up in the old, and resist possibilities of new vibrational levels. Examine your patterns and tell yourself the Truth!

This is a challenging point in time for dedicated relationship partner(s). Self-deceptions with illusion at work can mask the realities needed for Detachment. You need to face up to this if preparing to Move On!

Hosting Your Ego.

At some point, there is a crossroad.
You can consciously decide to host lower level Ego patterns,
... or to host the Higher Vibrations of Spirit.
Your choice, Friends.

Certain EGO patterns I mention relate to *default places that the mind will wander into, often times during periods where focus on particulars is not required, ... a <u>time fostering an idle mind and the precipice that lurks!</u>*

You may find it helpful, *when these patterns, defaults, and idle periods are in play, to **consciously shift** into actively Being Grateful and owning the new possibilities and activities that are opening up. Writing out a list of new, <u>'present time possibilities'</u> to fill the 'gap' can lubricate the way forward with added ease and grace. Focus upon your intentions and visions, hopes and dreams, why not be bold here?*

This is my list of new 'Present Time <u>Possibilities</u> <u>as of</u>   (date)

_____
_____
_____
_____
_____
_____
_____
_____
_____
_____
_____

_____
_____
_____
_____

In concert with this conscious shift, Our Divine Decrees can be of great assistance *to neutralize idle mind periods, and to hold them in alignment, in the neutral zone of emotion, or better yet into the positive zone.*
Wistful idleness *in this process of Detachment can engulf Human thought, tempting a slip backwards into the negative zone of emotion; such regression of consciousness, giving <u>fuel to a sustained Attachment. Forward motion, can be nicely managed and accelerated</u> by saying Decrees during appropriate periods, brief or extended, allowing your mind to alternatively drift into a conscious silence of rest, surrender and healing.*

In addition to forwarding your Detachment with Love Process, beautiful and heart-touching Decrees can give you *instant comfort, peace of mind, alignment, and bliss, ... if you will allow.*

You are supported and encouraged to welcome into your consciousness the daily power of *Decrees and Affirmations*, <u>specifically by memorizing them.</u> The time is now! Start with the easy ones first, and then the longer Decrees in a few weeks. Do you know any Decrees by heart?

Decree

Present Time

Once in each moment of present time,

My Christed self I do align,

In these my moments of reverie,

Upspring the joys I choose to be.

Alpha through Omega and

All that's between,

I AM in God's Light,

My Freedom is seen.

Violet Fire

Violet Fire thou love Divine
Blaze in this Heart of Mine
Thou are Mercy Forever True
Keep me always in tune with You.

The Presence

I AM that I AM

I AM that I AM

Oh GOD I know that

I AM that I AM

I AM I AM Beholding ALL

Mine Eye is single as I Call

Oh Raise Me Now and Set Me Free

Thy Holy Presence Now to BE.

                                      Om (A-u-m) mmmmm

In The Light

I AM GOD's Light

I feel my Love

As now I don

Thy Holy Glove

I AM the hand of God in action

Gaining victory every day

My pure Soul's great satisfaction

Is to walk the middle way

Once in each moment of present time

My Christed Self I do align

In these My moments of reverie, Up

spring the joys I choose to BE

Fill Me with Light, blaze Me bright,

And I will Be with Freedom alight.

Decreeing with OM

he Sacred sound of Om is here to assist you in effortlessly melding your consciousness into the pulse of GOD's Universes.

Freely breathe in and exhale the essence of the words in your own rhythm, tuning your voice and breath to merge yourself with the Eye of GOD. Seeing near and afar with your third eye will render your consciousness into an amazing proximity with the *enlightened perspective abilities* We wish for you. Receive the Blessing in Love.

As you begin your meditation, allow your mantra to drift your mind into a *conscious silence* of daily rest and healing. ***Daily practice*** I ask.

WE are with you always and pray for your alignment with the Will of God which I hold and anchor for Mankind in My Blue Ray, the First Ray of the Holy Spirit. May your life be in Divine alignment always.

El Morya Through Jah Rahn Ananda

LIGHT FOR THE SOUL

El Morya Transmission
Through Lah Rahn Ananda

Prayer of Divine Moments

Lead me, oh my sweet Lord, to choose thy bounty forever, for I know it is my destiny. Let me now hear your inspirations' love that guides me to make the most from each of our moments together, for I AM one with Thee.

As your child I stand in awe of the Divined free-will gift bestowed upon me and entrusted into my care. Guide me to heartfully know thy will as I carefully choose each of my new *moments. My right choices shall be the walk of my dharma that I demonstrate in full view of the ALL, for I AM one with Thee.*

May I forever embrace the lessons of my moments which I know embody my own choices. Grace me, Lord, with true perception of my every moment, though parts be bittersweet as I may choose to perceive. Let me see that I am blessed by all of my lessons, for I AM one with Thee.

Oh give me the awakened remembrance of my own Divine Self that reveals the true identity of Me to me in your likeness, for I AM one with YOU.

Let my will be your will forever and forever, oh my sweet Lord. Guide the steps of my walk to be trustworthy in the eyes of ALL. I pray to ignite the violet flame in the altar of my heart within each one of my newly treasured and joyfully shared moments with Thee. I AM your inspired instrument of Divine heart that chooses in love our moments together, for I AM so in love with YOU Oh my sweet Lord, my CREATOR.

EL MORYA
Through Lah Rahn Ananda   2001

Chapter 18

Moving On

After all is said and done, what comes next?

S**avoring lasting joys and healing of past wounds clearly seeks your conscious and focused efforts to complete,** resolve, and fully understand the big picture surrounding Spirit's part in creating your life-lesson(s). For your own Self-love, appreciate Spirit's purpose in bringing you the gifts of these important evolvement lessons, and *your opportunity*

269

... to mine the gold of Mastery!

To begin, know that your Gratitude, Forgiveness and Love are wondrous catalysts to Moving On. Put them into your daily tool box and make good use, Dear Friends.

NOW ... let Us focus on Forgiveness and on the reality of <u>all</u> the pieces of the puzzle, not just <u>your own</u> version.

> *Let you not always dignify your experience as the absolute Truth of the matter!*

Putting One's self in the shoes of another can bring marvelous insights of compassion, and Light up the way to <u>transcending</u> those past *detachment and reactivation issues to be resolved and behind you.*

Healing techniques may involve processing with yourself directly (if you are able), or processing with the support of a Spiritual channel, professional counselor, friend, etc. as well.

We are dealing with fundamentals here, including:

- <u>Accepting Reality of this moment</u>.

- Trusting that Spirit will guide you.

- Realizing you cannot rewrite history or the past, as those eggs have already been scrambled!

- Realizing *you have a choice to change* your consciousness and belief system in this present moment.

- Knowing you can change your outlook about past issues of stuckness by *consciously mining the gold of the life's lesson, here and now.*

- Accepting *each life's lesson as a sacred gift.*

- Being present to know that the *circumstance that brought the lesson to you is only delivered in this way, and done for a purpose.* **You are concentrating here on** *applying the lesson that the circumstance tool delivered!*

- *Staying open to this discovery,* which can lead you nicely to *completions and to letting go of the Reactivation behavior* that has lingered in your mind, especially during those idle mind periods.

- Being aware that you are now in control of this **Moving On** process, mainly through your choices.

- Opening yourself to Visions, new plans to fill in old gaps with future events, and *refreshing your life with new empowering interests* that open new space for joy, Love and happiness, and for you to MOVE ON!

Also in tandem, remember <u>after</u> you have done your part of the work, … to give to Spirit your moving on scenarios that are stuck, and ask us to take them and dissolve them for you in our Ascended Realm. Prayers aside, We will determine when your part of the work is sufficient.

We gladly serve in this capacity, <u>once you have done your work</u>. This is a Blessing We offer when Ones reach the full capacity of their powers and require a boost from Above with Our Love.

☙❧

Mining the Gold of your Life's Lessons.

List some life lessons here, and how you will be applying them to your expanding consciousness:

_____
_____
_____
_____
_____
_____
_____
_____
_____
_____
_____

_____
_____
_____
_____
_____
_____
_____
_____
_____
_____
_____
_____
_____
_____

Your Moving On Process.

We send you Blessings to be fully healed in the earlier *Detachment with Love* phase, to now enter a restored condition that will allow Moving On.

This includes being present, aware, appropriately detached, ... a condition of BEING restfully alert and Blissful in the midst of Change.

It is so true that Moving On in the midst of change is, by its very nature, challenging, confrontational and often seemingly devastating, *as you walk to Master the Human condition.*

Think of it this way: *Mastery of Change is a centerpiece of your evolvement. 'These Moving-On changes' are one aspect of this larger centerpiece picture.*

There is an old saying, perhaps Russian in origin,

"If you want to make an omelet, you have to break the eggs!"

**When you truly believe that all of a relationship's milestones have been passed through, along the road, and your Higher-self tells you your life's lessons here have been taught, then comes your choice!
You can give back to the Universe and Spirit your Attachments to outcomes gone bye ...** *from the heart level ... and feel the unparalleled experience of newly found FREEDOM in Moving On!*
Trust Us on this!

Whether Detaching from a long term committed Attachment and relationship investment, or simply 'un-hooking a hookup' as you would say, you will find completion, peace, and a new Freedom when you follow some basic fundamentals of moving on.

First, We recommend that you celebrate with gratitude all of the joys you have *given, received and shared back and forth during the course of this relationship time period, brief or lengthy, or somewhere in the middle.*

Next, create new interests, and connections to fill in the 'gap' and the empty space that you may be feeling, yes? We understand the Human feelings. Opportunities and Possibilities abound when Your *Newly Found Freedom is available and ready to fly, released from it's shackles*!

One of your famous Earthly Greeks reminds you that: **'Fortune Favors the Bold'**.

Remember, you are not alone, Dear Ones! **With Spirit imbedded as your Partner, you are One with the Universal Mind.** Spirit is on-line 24 x 7 to dynamically assist you in your aligned ventures forward. In full alignment, you can tap into the possibilities of the ALL and recreate joys and beauty that may have eluded you before new visions became apparent in your surrendered Moving-On process.

In the end, when all is said and done, allow yourself the joys of remembering the finest relationship moments you shared, holding them dearly in Gratitude, as flames of eternal Love, alive and well. Be at Peace and Move On wisely with My Blessings in the Light,

Saint Germain

Through Lah Rahn Ananda aka Gordon Corwin II

Chapter 19

Gratitude

To My Friends walking your path.

As you allow Ascended Spirit to enlighten and expand the veins of your consciousness, I as the Author, Channel and now one of Lord Saint Germain's Earth-partners, invite you to please join me in reciprocating the deepest possible gratitude for the very wonders of the Creator's Universe itself, and for the infinite brilliance embodied in this interconnecting structure throughout the highest Dimensions of Universal Consciousness.

God and Spirit have so ingeniously interwoven, as ONE, an amazing, infinitely organized hierarchical structure of Ascended Beings and timeless wisdom, allowing us on Earth to receive purifying transmissions from Above in real time, as they are continuously and effortlessly sent to Humanity. In my Channelship and role as a Partner of Spirit, I AM most grateful to serve as a minute part of this wondrous network of Spirit and Light, receiving for you the highest vibrational Octaves of Universal Truth.

In more simple terms, this is gratefulness for delivery of our Divinely guided tool-set for living 'The Grand Process' in this lifetime of self-transformation, awake and aware.

You may know that individual Ascended Masters carry their own unique energy, style, and color, delivering that segment of the Whole, which is their Ray of assigned specialty. And yet, ironically, these Beings are fully aligned, integrated, amalgamated, and enfolded into the greater Whole as ONE. I AM personally grateful that this demonstration of transcended Oneness from Above displays doorways to Unity consciousness and then God Consciousness for all of us.

My dream is for you to find these Saint Germain books to be your Personal Spiritual Guidebooks, leading you to experience the perfection of God's Grace, as you walk through your own doorways arched with inset stones of timeless wisdom.

Saint Germain's latest books, "VICTORY FOR THE SOUL, Relationships That Work", ... "THE SAINT GERMAIN CHRONICLES COLLECTION, A *Journey into Practical Spirituality*", ...and RISING ABOVE, *A Journey To Higher Dimensions* contain energies emanating from *several* different Ascended Masters to whom I AM immensely grateful. Please join me in the most heartful acknowledgment of: Lords Saint Germain, El Morya, Buddha, Hilarion, Mighty Victory, Jesus Sananda, Lady Portia, Lady Nada, Mother Mary, Archangels Michael, Zadkiel, Gabriel, and countless enlightened Beings, all standing to serve when called.

May Spirit's Grace crown your consciousness.

Love and Blessings,

Lah Rahn aka Gordon Corwin II

Chapter 20

Introduction to Changing Competition Into Oneness

A New Perspective and Paradigm

From Above, We see a new Paradigm being born among Humans, where Win-Win relationships of <u>ONENESS</u> will evolve into reality, replacing Win-lose Competition around your Globe. We admire this event! This starts the cycle of terminating Separation sourced by Competition in favor of Win-Win Outcomes For All. Behold My Friends! The time to join this new movement is now, Dear Ones! This empowering new <u>Paradigm</u> shift is ripe and ready for the picking!

❧❧

AUTHOR's FINALOGUE NOTE

Here, Saint Germain and I, Lah Rahn Ananda, His appointed instrument and partner, prepare to close this channeled, Wisdom-laced book about solving the puzzle of Human Relationships, ... *'Victory for the Soul, Relationships that Work'* ... embracing mysterious aspects of Being Human and living together in the energy of Oneness. Here is a Finalogue aspect which merits your kind attention in this moment.

This new Paradigm and Perspective, <u>Changing Competition into Oneness</u>, is one that Saint Germain has been patiently waiting in the Ethers to deliver, ... waiting to reveal to Mankind at the opportune moment. I note that this topic is an itch for Saint Germain that has gone unscratched... until now!

Treat yourself to this final Chapter 20 of Saint Germain's Ascended Wisdom, empowering and first of its kind. This Chapter is focused on *altering Mankind's own Perception and dominating use of competition* among Humans living in separation versus harmonizing in the Oneness of Relationships.

As you will, open your mind and heart to this revealing and enlightening piece, here now *to guide you as a participant in shifting modern Earth-life behavior,* where outmoded Win-lose outcomes are transcended and replaced by Win-Win vibrations for All.

This particular Chapter about Competition will also be published *under separate cover, for distribution to Spirit-seekers and Chelas who would dare to walk this exciting new path in harmony, Love, and celebration of others in your every-day lives.*

Enjoy this refreshing journey into a *New Paradigm and wave of Synchronicity, a ripe Perspective poised to change the quality of Human Life!*

Love,
   Lah Rahn Ananda,
      Oceanside, CA
            Lah@SaintGermainChronicles.com

☙❧

Chapter 21

Changing Competition Into Oneness
A New Perspective and Paradigm

As Lord Saint Germain, I come to you from The Ascended Spirit Realm to <u>bring forth a much needed new perspective for Humanity about replacing the Competition consciousness that pervades throughout your World.</u> Yes, this is a long overdue correction, and indeed a daunting one, given Humanity's track record of a massively intransigent Ego, collective and individual! With this Paradigm comes a magnificent new opening to ongoingly celebrate the Oneness that We Truly are!

And now, We must All look carefully to see where this Paradigm shift must start! It starts with you as an individual, spreading to groups of individuals, and then onward into the collective! This shift of consciousness is part of the overall course and process of evolving your individual consciousness to embrace a Journey into Practical Spirituality, embracing its axioms and refinements. *This new Paradigm is one such crucial refinement to be now included in your journey,* Folks!

Individually, as Light Workers, Chelas, and Spirit-seekers, you have a Golden opportunity to distinguish yourself as pillars of *this new Paradigm of Oneness*, a long awaited wave of advancement for the Human Global consciousness. And yes, this higher level of enlightenment may take Humanity three or four succeeding generations to bring about … *to fully make this shift into a full reality.*

Notice the broad scope of this Paradigm. Although We focus primarily here on the blatant competition raging in your World at large, … remember to broaden your scope *to perceive the entire picture, including your personal picture*! This would include competition on a *more intimate level*, perhaps between spouses or siblings or children, or co-workers, or even superiors at times! *As We proceed together to unfold this transmission, hold this broader scope in mind and consciousness, … to get the full impact of My gift of Wisdom.*

With your engagement, as individuals working in the Light, Win-Win Relationships among Mankind, across your Globe will light the way to overcome the ruthless separation and obsessive domination now in use through a devastating Worldwide custom. The tradition of competition in place as it is now, unmercifully pulverizes so many worthy participants along the paths of their life-streams.

As We in Ascended Spirit continue to monitor Mankind** in various aspects of present day consciousness, it is quite apparent that HUMANITY, over millennia of Earth time, has *evolved into this unaligned and seriously damaging aspect of relationship, with the rampant energies of Competition in place, as you can see!*

As Man has evolved over the eons, He has sadly failed to mold and shape the *original* use of Competition *into what could now be a powerful Blessing* to All modern Mankind, around the Globe. Here is the opportunity to set this consciousness straight, individually and collectively!

So, to begin with, let Me point out and reveal to you some insights. All of Humanity on a global basis has gradually grown over the eons to regard *competition as* an accepted behavior. Rather than satisfying the original drive for survival, as in the beginning, this *behavior has morphed into a mechanism that now feeds the Egos of Mankind*. Read on and you will possibly gain new insights.

This current judgment-based behavior standard ... of *better than and less than* ... has been historically agreed upon by most all of Mankind. Be aware that this ruthless practice has been set in stone for centuries. Many of you have observed this and squirmed in anguish about what to do, yes? Do I have your attention?

Win-Lose. In your World today, you will notice in your own life-stream how very differently all of Human-kind will choose to relate. Some will 'Be' an overall Oneness with the energies and capabilities of others, *embracing differences* with enthusiasm, welcoming and celebrating the *individual capabilities* among the Brotherhood of Mankind. Others continue to be duped into following the accepted, status quo standard of competition favoring win-lose behavior, using instilled judgments that hold Mankind in separation's firm grip that strangles!

Participation of Personal Bests. Here now, We Above are All about Humanity evolving into a higher vibration of Oneness with this new Paradigm, where Personal Bests are coupled with <u>true relationships in celebration with fellow participants in your arenas of Human life.</u>

As Truth unfolds about Oneness, the energy of competition fades away as superfluous Ego food that has no meaning among enlightened Beings!

In this Paradigm of loving energy in Oneness, there is no presence of envy, jealousy, or judgment of others performance. There is simply a feeling of unity and common bond as an individual participates in life's events, showing up with One's personal best and <u>being responsible to one's self to accept the 'what is' outcome of these moments as 'what is meant to Be'</u>.

With this energy wrapped around One's *full and dedicated participation* in various life's events, a sense of FREEDOM and inner satisfaction is born within. This is then reinforced with showers of Spirit's Love and synchronicity, sourced by vibrations anchored in Our Lairs. Some of you have already experienced multiple synchronicities, and occasionally in one day of Earth time!

<u>**When you individually surrender to the best of you**, and fully engage in authentic participation of togetherness and commonality, thoughts and behaviors of Win-lose COMPETITION are erased before they start.</u>

Now you have another color of FREEDOM to add to your consciousness, … a superlative gift of Spirit, a state of Being that you have well earned! … another arrow in your quiver of enlightenment!

MAKING THE TRANSITION

C**hanging into this state of consciousness**, where you have a new relationship with full participation of Oneness in common with others, … is a grand and courageous step forward through your sometimes dog-eat dog World today, … believe Me, I understand your plight! I have compassion! And I also have inspiration for those who will CHANGE! Read on, Dear Ones.

Be joyful in this new relationship and acknowledge yourself when you have made this shift of consciousness with a deep sigh of relief, having let go of one of man's oldest negative habits of behavior, ...that would be supporting Competition that produces winners and losers rather than a Win-Win for everyone participating at their personal best.

Now about self-honesty. I hasten to add that at this point you need to be *brutally honest with yourself* about full participation. This means that you are wholeheartedly in the game, prepared to show up fully, *with all of your capabilities in hand*, brought to bear, and <u>without excuses</u> for failing to cut the mustard, or to maximize your own individual capabilities. There is no halfway allowed for those who would receive the

Blessings of **FREEDOM from Competition**, as I will now describe.

Yes, your new journey into Freedom can now be launched with this level of participation, one where you completely accept the outcome of your participation and the sometimes unfortunate judgments of those in power, ... judges that would rank and reward you according to the rules that We are all about to change!

Such an evolved consciousness now introduces a guiding light of truly Being *as you deliver your own unique individual capabilities.* And yes, your pesky Earth customs may continue to have their way, for a time, as they resist change. Let patience be your friend.

This old and worn out arena of relationships that I speak of is where *'winners' are glorified* as superior (often without regard to merit in the eyes of Spirit) and where *'losers' are shamed and denigrated* (by those who judge, even **possibly by you, before you change!**) Also, beware that *you as an individual may be tempted, before your Paradigm change, to judge yourself as unworthy when present competition per se is your guide!*

And there is much to this game of Change! I invite you to consciously intake the energies that surround your new Freedom a*nd* Joy of sharing yourself in this exciting way. You need to know that beyond sharing just your capabilities in life's events of relationship, you now have entry into the Domain of Love, which can expand your experiences of Oneness. These realities can lead you to transcend *competitions of old,* possibly *focused upon <u>defeating</u> others in favor of <u>Win-Win Oneness for All.</u>*

And yes, I acknowledge that Outcomes of your participation will, at this point in time, be sometimes seen sadly judged by your World, which We together are about to change in this way, …with your engagement. *Meanwhile, the significance of outcomes can be chosen to be as they are in the space of the Earth-World, and you have the power to choose differently inside the space of your own Personal Universe!*

This new Domain of Oneness carries you into a Love vibration, where you can join with others, … in your own authentic way, … your true inner feelings that you will have throughout your mind, body and heart, as you participate in this Paradigm of Oneness.

At this juncture, there comes a peaceful knowingness. Enjoy the ride! As you share this new Paradigm with others who also practice and participate as well, *you all will begin to feel the new energy in common, and with a pleasant sense of gratification, centered in your heart and crown chakras.* This sensation will be very *meaningful to yourself and to others*, once your feelings of Oneness are exposed through your living and when others can clearly see this in you.

Also, look for the automatic response in your thoughts, words and *actions as your default behaviors around Earthly competition* are fading away as old and now worn out. In the new mindset of participating together vs. competing to defeat, there is great inward satisfaction waiting for you!

Peaceful knowingness coupled with a vibration of Love will take you far, while you authentically share, and sometimes display, your skills and capabilities throughout the arenas of life.

THE ZONE OF ONENESS

You have, in this context, now entered the zone of 'Oneness in Relationship'. You are harmoniously sharing your abilities, in this particular context, with those who share a common interest in the activity at hand.

About Relationships, ... please regard this new book about Relationships that Work, "VICTORY FOR THE SOUL", Amazon 2022 Gordon Corwin II ... *as practical Spiritual Wisdom that guides you through expansive Truths that uncover unknown nuances of personal relationships: individual, group, and the grand collective alike.*

Alright! As you are embraced by this new zone of consciousness, focus on your participation with others in events using your common skills together (the sports arena is only an example).
Once in this zone, you have *internalized Relationships in a new way, and viscerally imbedded the Win-Win philosophy and practice into your thinking and new behavior. You have transcended emotions of envy and jealousy of others with different capabilities. You will be connected to Spirit and to your Higher-self in a heart space of open caring and sharing, that amplifies your whole experience into a new crescendo.*

In this zone, you will have transcended the *quite honorable behavior of simply 'Being Nice'*. **Are you with me?**

BE at inner peace as you 'live this vibration, in this space (zone) inside of your life from this day forward'. <u>You</u>

are now joined Above, beyond the separation mindset ... fading into the background of all things gone by.

While Ascension itself requires a multitude of transmutations in the consciousness of an Earth life, this **Milestone of Oneness** is a truly basic part of your Divine and Grand Process of **Ascension training in this lifetime**, including showing up in this grand fashion from this day forward, for the remainder of your Earth days!

Read and re-read the foregoing page and allow it to penetrate. Lord Jesus Sananda will assist you if you ask nicely. Sananda and I are Divinely joined at the hip as you may recognize by now!

MAKING REQUESTS TO BE CHOSEN

Here lies yet another key aspect for your Earthly scenario of awareness. It is about the mindset of viewing Oneness versus Separation with regard to your Requests to be Chosen.

Such requests, for your clarity here, include presenting yourself to others for selection ... to individuals, groups, companies, etc.. With this very act of presenting yourself as you fully participate in your current life on the stage of Planet Earth, *there will be occasions where you Request to be Chosen.* **The outcomes of these requests will entail the free-will choices of those who would choose.**

As Humans, choosers are granted the power of free-will choice in a free-will World. Winners are commonly chosen because they prevailed in <u>competition</u> and defeated losers. Can you see We are headed toward a fundamental distinction in this discussion?

We Above want you to make a distinction here between the *mindset of <u>'being chosen'</u>* versus <u>*the mindset of sheer competition with judgment*</u> *to produce a 'winner in victory' and by default, commonly a loser(s) in defeat.*

In the beginning, Our creator embraced Humanity in particular, to carry the phenomenon of Free-will. This can be viewed as a privilege or a burden with responsibilities, ... or both, if you choose. Not All other Beings in the Universe enjoy such a grand privilege, nor its responsibilities and consequences regarding outcome of choice.

And here We point out to you the *Free-will privilege* of choosing, and how it can be carried out with no required judgment involved at any level... just simply "I choose vanilla" and "I am not making strawberry wrong". Do you see?

And so goes CHOOSING a participant who requests to be CHOSEN! This could be you looking for a job opportunity, etc.

STARK SURVIVAL ... IN THE BEGINNING

In the beginning, your plant and animal kingdoms and early forms of human life were all focused upon providing for their survival. In some cases the resources and means for survival were limited. There was competition for all in various greater or lesser ways. When food and shelter, for example, were within *easy* reach for all Humans, abundance produced a more relaxed atmosphere. There was lesser need for constant competition in order to survive while surrounded with some abundance.

However, when the scenario shifted into some degrees of *scarcity*, competition raised its head, and the game changed! Clearly, competition is a *primal urge-driven* behavior for your various Earthly kingdoms of living things, plant, animal, Human, bacterial, etc.

However, with the advent of Mankind, and with growth of consciousness that began to exceed survival needs, *We Above have noticed for eons that the urge for Human survival has become drastically convoluted into urges of the Human Ego.*

As Mankind has evolved, the Human Ego has grown exponentially to regard competition for survival as much more than just that, *but as a vehicle to satisfy the dominating urges and demands of the Ego.* For example, these demands are *commonly supported by judgments* as: better than, lesser than, superior to, greater than, more powerful than, ... badges often worn by competitors in domination obsessed arenas.

EGO DRIVEN PERSPECTIVES

Perspectives of Oneness and Separation. Let us take a look at some various perspectives that Humans now hold in their illusion about how relationships are meant to function.

First and foremost, Human ego drives all of you, in some way or another, to create wants to be judged the winner, to be right, and often times to be recognized as 'better than' or the best! We are focused upon the role that competition has assumed by Mankind and which needs massive <u>change to shift into alignment</u>.

Can you see where this is going? *Long ago, Humanity began heading down the road of a Win-lose perspective emphasizing competition.*

Little do most of you know that this is one of the lowest vibrational octaves available among your choices of Being in your 3rd Dimension of Consciousness ... and that there are almost always Win-Win solutions that can alternatively prevail in the Light.

Even though survival drives may be basically satisfied, *can you see how your world is designed by MANKIND itself, <u>to persist in regarding multiple situations as predominantly Win-lose?</u>*

Look for example at your sports structures *where a winner is highlighted over a loser, and this perspective ignores <u>the possibility of all participants being winners in their own right</u>. Competition fosters the illusion of rewarding Win-lose outcomes where competition is in play.*

Can you see how *this choice of Perspective about competition has invaded the Human consciousness to <u>exclude</u> recognizing* *people and things that are not <u>labeled and judged</u> as winners?* There is a Free-will choice of Oneness energy that has unfortunately been sacrificed by Mankind for *a lower human vibration,* <u>**where competition is to glorify the winner and crush the loser as inferior, and often ignored, having been judged by rules of Mankind.**</u>

Examine, if you will, common behaviors upon your Earth plane in your sporting events. Humanity has agreed to be judged by the rules of competition as producing a glorified winner or inferior loser. What is possible here is for all to <u>emerge with a sense of Oneness</u> with satisfaction over separation.

In the design of the Earthly stage for Humans to reside upon, We in Spirit alongside God Above intentionally created and placed the *phenomenon of Duality* to accompany the blessing of Human Free-will choice. <u>With this comes the test</u> for all Humans, including even you today in your daily life. One of the tests here, in this context, is to mold your Perspective about competition into a clear objective of: *<u>'we can all win', leaving</u>* <u>negative Duality choices behind. Everyone who fully</u> *participates in good faith can transcend and chose to be a* <u>winner within their Personal Universe having done their personal best.</u>

PARTICIPATION AT YOUR BEST!

P**articipation within your Personal Universe**. The fact that you participated, and did your best gives you basis for *transcending the win-lose philosophy within your own consciousness*. Having absolutely done your

very personal best gives you an opening to transcend negative judgments of others and still see reality!
Within your own heart, can you know satisfaction and personal reward in the fact that you did your personal best on a certain occasion? Of course, this is your choice!

The fact that you participated and didn't quit when the going got tough, is so much more to your credit. You may have failed to achieve *your objective* using one strategy, but then you develop another which was/is in alignment and, at a minimum, brings you harmony?

So where do we go with all of this, as guidance for those of you starting out in life and for those in midstream or perhaps in your twilight years? We have some suggestions for you about how you can hold the perspective of competition that will serve your consciousness, mind, body and Soul.

Respect yourself. Take the opportunity to respect yourself for those times when you have done your absolute personal best. Give yourself the opportunity to be fully satisfied and rewarded when your performance is 100% or greater than you believe to be your maximum. *Next, knowing in your heart that your personal best is whatever that is, and a comparison of your best to another's best is just an outcome turned into a judgment of 'better than' or 'less than'.* **Remember, with respect to good and bad, ... there is only what IS!**

And there you have it, My Friends, you have a choice in your heart-space of how you regard **Participation in Oneness vs. competition.** You recognize that in the Earth-world (outside of your personal Universe) there may appear to be dog eat dog feasting frenzies ... to which you do not choose to belong! You further recognize the simple facts of how Mankind has evolved up to now, and that you yourself do not necessarily need to be a part of the herd.

BE THE DEMONSTRATION

So let's be specific. **You are a swimmer participating in a swim meet.** If you are scheduled to swim in a certain way or certain distance, you will typically be compared to other swimmers. And at the end of your races, there will be judged winners and there will be others judged in lower rankings. Competition is common.

Look at your great football leagues and all of the glorified importance of winning and winning more, ad infinitum! Winning teams are glorified and losing teams are known to have members openly *shedding tears of disgruntled and denigrated Egos,* including crippling esteem issues, ... as recipients of competition judgments (both from *without and often from within*).

Be a Leader by Demonstration. You have the opportunity to be one of the Ones who leads the way to *transcend this old way of Being,* <u>to raise the quality of your life, and move up higher and higher on the Spiritual ladder at the same time!</u> Knowing that you have participated in arena activities that are often competitive, you can choose to now display your best and Be willing to accept the outcome in two ways.

1. *Within the personal universe inside yourself,* as I've pointed out, Being at peace with your Personal Best.
2. And yes, in the *universe outside of yourself,* you can also accept the outcomes as 'what is at this time' according to the rules of others in judgment.

It would be foolhardy to say you are *unaffected by the judgment of those outside of your personal universe, and yet in the 5th and 7th or 9th Dimensions, you are willing to transcend these emotions and their judgements, even knowing the way that the system <u>currently</u> works.*

We Above are working with people in your very shoes to bring change to your World. You can, within your own personal Universe, give due to your personal recognition of All those who participate and do their very level best. Some participants will belong to a 'society of winners' whom you recognize, whom you care for, and with whom you share the venue. And yet, your mindset allows you to be at peace with your BEST! <u>In this evolved mindset, could you not simply skip the tears drama and move on?</u>

Now, with this new viewpoint, *with this new perspective about participation,* is it not possible for you to go out into the world and be a new person in relationship to competition? *Is that not possible?*

I say enroll yourself in this healthy outlook on life and you too will reap the glory whatever the outcome, and benefit in the joys of knowing that you can be a <u>*winner as your best*</u>, aside from those who may judge you!

Hold this guidance in your belief system as sacred. *It will serve you well.* Be <u>**willing to let go of your attachment to the importance of being ranked and judged by others when you yourself know you have performed at your personal best.**</u>

With these axioms in mind, you can enjoy a new serenity and peace of mind that you may have never expected. I pray that you will. I pray that you will honor yourself. Love yourself, and see through this part of the *Human Illusion* that says participation must be viewed as competition, structured exclusively around win and lose energies.

GETTING STARTED IN A NEW DIMENSION

So, My Dear Friends, are you ready to begin? Well, living your lives as Spirit-seekers, this all begins with you! *Individually, this new, refined energy of participation at your personal best alongside your colleagues whom you support versus competing to defeat others ... is the name of this new game!*

Can you see this new Relationship Perspective has many of the elements of acceptance, kindness, Love, acknowledgment and reward *without* **the degradation and negativity that glorifies some and crushes others.**

Your newfound energy of *Participation as your Best*, will spread throughout arenas of those with whom you associate and participate! And you will be surprisingly well-received by individuals who would be uplifted and empowered along with you. *This wave of energy can spread* through families, friends, Colleges, Universities, amateur and professional sports leagues, to larger groups, institutions, countries and nations ... toward a shift in the collective consciousness at large.

With devotion, this ripple effect will then have its positive way for Mankind ... *if you will only begin the movement as an individual. Like evolvement of overall consciousness, this particular facet of your character must start with strength of character, dedication, and clarity. Individuals then ripple their way into the collective and then We have Change for the highest and best good! Do you see?*

I, Lord Saint Germain, <u>will support, honor and reward those who march to this beat for participation with others without judgment.</u> You can count on me. I AM One of you!

I will support and empower you hand and glove to be your best in your life *and to <u>demonstrate</u> this new relationship of participation* to replace the outmoded earthly custom of win-lose competition, ... <u>a judgment behavior sadly and widely held and accepted in illusion by Mankind, by its own self-propelled customs, by structures and by ego-based behaviors.</u>

And, do not blame this sad condition of Earthly win-lose competition upon Earth's Duality ... a further test brought by Our Creator, ... which elicits your aligned free-will with choices to transcend, ... if you have the nerve and conviction and the *grit*! Duality per se will be reserved for discussion on another day, Friends!

Yes indeed, this New Perception is a big change in the making. Several generations of Human lifetimes gone by will be required, yes, and *this is a test for you individually.* Are you up to the task?

And yes, this is a test for the collective to see if it and when it will accede to the higher evolution of individuals like yourselves and *abandon it's own ways which foster separation.*

This new perception is also a test of the collective to *now mirror individual changes evolving here into a collective reflection of that evolvement!*

With Joy and enthusiasm from above, I embrace you in this brave and daring pursuit. Let me hear from you as these days of *Relationship in Oneness* pass through your lives, and as you proceed on to your successes in this life-stream!

Purification of the Human mind is massively essential to reach the higher Vibration, you may seek. *These distinctions I make to you in nearly every transmission are keys to open* *gateways through which you can walk, once these distinctions are clearly and fully Mastered.*

The process of installing this new Paradigm of Relationship in Oneness *entails awareness of its relation to the fundamentals of your own individual Grand Process, Folks.* You may recognize the elements of this Paradigm as *common to those appearing in your overall process of Belief System evolution in the grand sense.*

This Paradigm holds no exceptions, where alignment with Spirit continues to require attention to:

>Judgment temptations
>Free-will Choice
>Ego and Emotions
>Attachment and Detachment
>Resistance
>Surrender to What Is
>Willingness to Change
>Opportunities for FREEDOM
>Love, ... and much more.

Remember, once you have fully traveled through a Gateway and have achieved Mastery of a particular milestone in your Spiritual Journey, that portal need not be traversed again! This is the Milestone of Oneness.

Eventually, the final Golden doorway will appear *for those who are Chosen by the Lords of Karma to enter into My Domain and Kingdom of the Crystal Cave, ... your destination and encircled place of peace and rest for you always throughout Universal time.*

We Above All pray in Oneness that you, individually, will *rise to this occasion with great vigor, enthusiasm and*

celebration, gracefully displaying your progress with flying colors!

The outcome of this massive New Paradigm and movement will infuse the joy 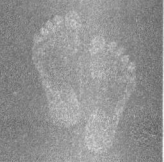 and FREEDOM, as Full Participation in Oneness becomes reality in your World and in Worlds beyond!

With great Joy and enthusiasm, I embrace you in this brave and daring pursuit. Let me hear from you as  these days of Relationship in Oneness pass through your lives, and as you proceed on to your successes! Heed My Wisdom, Dear Ones, and be well as you walk in the Light.

With My Blessings,
Saint Germain
    with Lah Rahn Ananda.

© Copyright 2022 Gordon W. Corwin II
ALL RIGHTS RESERVED INCLUDING THE RIGHT OF REPRODUCTION IN WHOLE OR IN PART IN ANY FORM.

Contact: Lah@SaintGermanChronicles.com

Chapter 21

Saint Germain's Inspiration to the Author

The inspiration to write this book gratefully came to me directly from Lord Saint Germain himself, with guidance for polishing up my own needed Personal Relationship skills through His channeled wisdom and guidance. And, as Divine destiny would have it, He also emphasized the massive need for all Humans to Master Relationship dynamics, ... as the hottest topic on the Planet Earth at this time. Thus, Saint Germain's Bootcamp Relationship Training episodes directed at yours truly over a three year time span, <u>gradually</u>

morphed, expanded and evolved into a full blown Saint Germain book, His second such work of its type to be released over His signature in the last 70 years. This work contains a multitude of commonly shared relationship issues that can largely apply to any Human, regardless!

Consequently, this book of Wisdom is truly inspired and born ... now to be shared as enlightenment training applicable to ALL on the Earth Globe.

Mining the Gold of Life's lessons along the way has been my highest priority all through the writing and channeling phases to co-create this book, "*VICTORY FOR THE SOUL, Relationships That Work*". The intent of Lord Saint Germain has been to capture and present common elements that seem to be deeply threaded through personal relationships, Globally challenging people of all cultures and races.

Since we are all ultimately One, and cut from the same cloth, the wisdom of these lessons is ubiquitous, and consequently useful on a wide scale across the obvious range of cultural differences among Humans. Minus the drama surrounding individual cases, I soon saw, as the channel/author, the enormous potential for many Spirit seekers to widely apply these building blocks and relationship essentials through the evolvement that Saint Germain offers here, an invaluable life's Blessing.

I soon learned that authenticity, being totally honest with myself in unfolding and refining this enlightened relationship process, is paramount. Diligently digging out the lessons with as much awareness as possible, has been enormously empowering for me *to get to bottom line Truths that emerge while examining relationships of all types.* Key and fundamental elements of personal relationships, as you may note in the Chapter titles chosen by Lord Saint Germain, expose deeply imbedded dynamics which ask for our focus.

I AM most grateful to Lord Saint Germain and All of the Ascended Realm to be chosen as the Spiritual channel to bring this book into the Earth World in His name and bearing his signature.

During the publishing of this book, there were some personal highlights that stand out. I can tell you of *four major life's lessons that have emerged for me.* Hopefully these will have meaning for you, starting with reading this book *and then applying the Wisdom to your own discovered life's lessons, as your daily life unfolds for the rest of this incarnation and beyond.*

First, **THE LESSON OF SELF LOVE** ... I learned that generosity has Boundaries! Getting clear on identifying and differentiating between *Wants and Needs applied to generosity!* Then, being clear about generously serving others in the highest way, while SIMULTANEOUSLY taking conscious care to honor myself and Not to Neglect My Own Needs of Self-Love. Also, I acknowledge, more than ever, the call to keep Love fires aflame around Detachments as they occur.

Second, **THE LESSON OF PATIENCE** ... I appreciate the many rewards of patience when I when I use more patience. In my case, as a type A personality, I know it is a learned skill. *When I can bring patience into the personal interaction,* sometimes even with emotions nagging away, the need for a *default* Ego reaction quickly evaporates, and *two inspirations take place for me*:

- to <u>find out more information (now) if I need it,</u> ... what may be missing ... before I choose.
- to <u>listen to my intuition and Spirit for the creative Win-Win solution(s)</u> *waiting for me to be considered*. I know there is a solution for every problem.

Third, <u>THE LESSON OF AGREEMENTS</u>. I Am now, more than ever, very careful to give consideration before Agreeing and committing, and then, once I agree, to *Fully and <u>willingly Own</u>* Agreements made ... this is a huge life's lesson for which I Am grateful. This ownership reminds me *that <u>I agree with myself to be freely willing</u> to carry out a promise I have made!*

Saying Yes or No. I Am more aware than ever that consideration includes thinking about all aspects, implications, and possible consequences before saying 'yes or no'. And there is the part of being fully honest with myself about saying yes or no. This I have learned and it needs practice. This part of the lesson is simply: if consideration says 'no' I must refrain from somehow acquiescing into saying 'yes', and have clarity about my convictions. I have learned to accept that sometimes a 'No' involves tough love, and requires my stepping up to the plate!

Fourth, and not least ... <u>**HANDLING SITUATIONS IN REAL TIME**</u>. When situations arise, with feelings sometimes intense, when we are at odds with each other, sometimes stuck in controversy or confusion, ... to *quietly and very openly speak the <u>candid Truth</u> of 'what is going on' in the moment*. This is so very helpful to defuse emotions and then to open *space for the Win-Win solution to come into play*. I Am Blessed to hear these Win-Win solution suggestions directly from my Higher-Self and Spirit as well, often with little or no effort, save my 'getting out of the way'. *I pray to always put higher wisdom into my life at the perfect times.*

For you, I wish all of these and more fine rewards to come your way. May you have joys, Blessings, Love and happiness that result from your newly found Masteries in Relationship, possibly some sourced from this book.

Finally, it is such a deep privilege for me to serve you and All of the Ascended Masters, Lord Saint Germain in particular, through the channeling and publishing this Book, done with my greatest of care and diligence deserving for All Humanity.

Love to you,

Lah Rahn

Chapter 22

Saint Germain's
QUOTATIONS

Victory for the Soul
Relationships that Work

Gaining Awareness
is the first step in your liberation from the Human Illusion.

Notice the sense of Freedom that you can generate when your priority fits the need!

Partnership

A confluent overlap of Consciousnesses between partners is a beautiful blending of energies sourcing a true relationship to be born, blossom, and thrive.

In Partnership, as in Your Own Grand Process, the middle or the end may or may not faintly resemble the beginning ... as Change has its way!

Celebrate and embrace your shared Love,
life's lessons learned, and Win-Win outcomes ... that
you create together as 'Us' in relationship.

About Desire, ... Truly *Being* in full-hearted, flourishing
relationship is for Ones with commitment,
and the faint of heart need look elsewhere.

Trust in Spirit when We say that
beyond your comfort zone
lies the space of evolved growth
and its potential rewards.

The power of enlightened teamwork and bonding,
through a mindset of Us and We, is a trustable asset to
anchor relationships of all types.

As surely as individuals make up their partnership in union, they can also maintain their own *appropriate* individual identities.

※

Perception

Let it be said that We are all bonded *together as One* in the grandest sense, albeit as Beings now in Ascended Spirit, or as you are now incarnated in Human flesh.

When Bonding is *intensified into a tightly held forever-binding* Attachment ... never ever to escape your clutch and grasp, ... know that you are obsessed and Bound!

The *'compromise', as a well-worn out solution,* is so common in your World, yet so deeply impregnated with an Earth-World consciousness that buys this Human Illusion as its flawed truth.

Being left dissatisfied or in emotional limbo casts its own shadow on the compromise just reached, even though 'agreed' upon.

Do your level best to take lifetime experiences and their outcomes in stride.

Drink the nectar from your life's lessons, Drop by Drop.

Patience

Moreover, *for Advanced Spiritual Beings* on the Earthplane, indulgence in anger-filled reactions is now an <u>Ego luxury</u> that you can ill afford.

You are wise from this moment forward to consider patience as <u>mandatory,</u> not an optional frivolity of your relationship.

Are you going to stay stuck INSIDE the upset or choose now to stand OUTSIDE of the upset viewing its reflection from a new perspective?

Patience is the catalyst that allows space for creation of Win-Win solutions!

Remember, rushing the process can have its consequences.

Patience is needed for
Divine Timing to incubate.

In the end, when all is said and done, allow yourself the joys of remembering the finest relationship moments you shared, holding them dearly in Gratitude, as flames of eternal Love, alive and well.

Change

Change will have *Its* W*ay, regardless.*

Being a Friend of Change will strengthen you in facing the inevitable.

Freely Allowing Change as it pops up in your life, is an attribute of consciousness for a person committed and empowered to pursue an examined Human Lifetime, leading to the ExtraOrdinary!

Change can be viewed from a number of different perspectives, as your consciousness and Ego will allow.

On the brighter side, changing times can be often welcomed by some as a refreshing manifestation of the new, beyond the Status Quo!

At some point there there is a crossroad ... to **host** your Ego and its antics <u>**or**</u> to **BE the host** of your Higher Dimensional Consciousness and Rise Above! Your choice.

Ego

Egos will try their best to hold you prisoner in the illusion that 'you are <u>always</u> right'.

The grizzly ingredients of an upset on fire within will easily fuel the 'always right Ego on duty'.

There is a high ransom, indeed, that Human Spirit of potential needs to pay for the stubborn and resolute self-indulgences of Narcissism.

Your Ego can hold you captive, shackled in its prison, if you choose.

Relationship Mastery requires discovering those default responses, packed tightly in your belief system, that will surely need to be jettisoned while Ego must pay the price of submission!

Resistance or surrender …
your obstacle or your miracle?

As a captive of your Ego,
your hands are tied.

Egos are reluctant if not deaf to the naked truth.

Resistance is a costly chosen behavior
when choice of Truth comes knocking!

☙❧

Truth and Illusion

Let you not always dignify *your experience* as the
absolute truth of the matter!

Opinions are only Opinions*!*

Illusion is at odds with the Truth and it is the grand
disguise that covers up!

Truly and fully *knowing yourself* disarms
self-deception and denial.

Self-talk   Self-Love

Being Truth is Self-Love.

Self-love leads you to find Peace within yourself.

Celebrate and embrace your shared love,
life's lessons learned, and Win-Win outcomes ... that
you create together.

And, where Love is yearned for,
perhaps it magically appears for you as the place you

have longed to enter … and you wonder why it has evaded you … and now here it is!

A healthy Self-talk dialogue can sing delightfully to the highest octave of your consciousness and make you smile, inside and out.

Be brutally honest with yourself about purifying your Self-talk thoughts, as Self-dishonesty results in an Ego deceiving a fool. Both are wasting their time!

In a sense your Self-Talk defines a large part of who you really are at the core level.

Similar to shifting *Judgments into NonJudgment*s … shifting *Attachment into Detachment is equally impactive* … when translated into <u>Detachment with Love.</u>

Once a delicate perspective of Balance is achieved
in some degree of Mastery,
happiness flows in to the mixture
like honey from the hive you have created!

Emotions

Trust in Spirit when We say that
beyond your comfort zone
lies the space of evolved growth
with its potential rewards.

To heal the *effect* of your own 'Triggers' is to heal the
vibration of your own Emotions.

The *One* who becomes angry has become a
captive of their own device!

Master your Emotions, and you can become a
Blessed Spiritual Observer
beyond the reach of Earthly anxieties.

Let the Emotions of Others be theirs
Without obligation to make them yours.

Communication

Put Ambiguity aside, Dear Ones,
And make your communications
Clear, crisp, and well-considered
Before your mouth shall have its way.

One face of you turns out to be the way you communicate.

Building Communication *skill*
Requires attention to your choice of words, and a focus upon their delivery
Where actions match your communications!

You can be Master of clear communications or let your communication *breakdowns* be the Master of you.

Communicating from the Heart in authentic Relationship delivers an even exchange of energy, positive and with Love.

Love, Compassion, and Forgiveness

Remember, Receiving is also part of the Grand Process, *and* you are Divinely entitled to receive when alignment, gratitude and Love are yours!

Choosing actions that generate Love, happiness and
Soul growth for others opens the portal for
The same energy flowing back unto you
... In kind!   Divine Reciprocity.

Half-assed approaches to relationship rarely bear
the fruit.

Saint Germain Quotations
From previous channelings

❧❧

Keen are the uses of adversity.

Develop the ability to discern without the
burden of Ego's judgments
being inserted into the mix.

Surrender Yourself to Truth and Reality
without compromising intention.

Use your Spiritual Toolbox
to flex and bend in the Third Dimension,
the 3-D of Earth consciousness.

Left and right together join the absolute and the relative.

Dig deeply for rewards of the Truth.

Willingly abide with the Truth about things and people ... without judgment ... and know Freedom.

Acknowledge Reality and engage in its uses.

A Master endorses recognition of Reality while allowing Free-will to be.

© Copyright 2022 Gordon W. Corwin II

ALL RIGHTS RESERVED
INCLUDING THE RIGHT OF REPRODUCTION
IN WHOLE OR IN PART IN ANY FORM.

Contact: Lah@SaintGermanChronicles.com

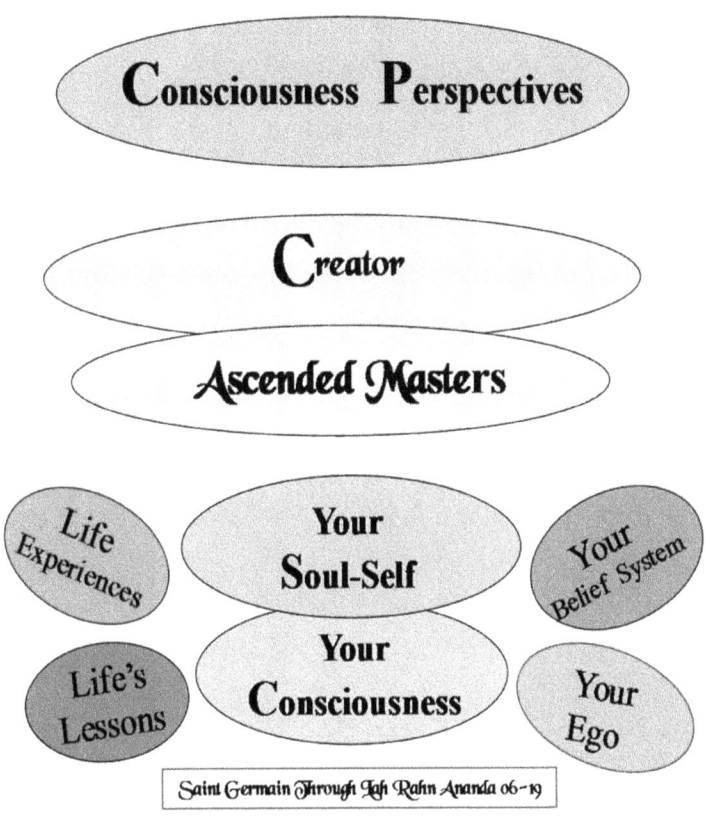

DISCLAIMER

The information contained within this Book is strictly for educational purposes. This Book and the Book's elements are provided to readers committed to Spiritual education, self-discovery, self-actualization, and transformation to align individual belief systems with a common source, Our Creator and Spirit, as the guiding light to enter doorways of change, new possibilities, growth, and manifestations within reach of an extraordinary and self-examined Human lifetime. Readers are encouraged to choose, of their own free-will and volition, to accept, to follow, or to reject the guidance, ideas, philosophies, stated truths, and techniques presented herein. If you wish to apply ideas and guidance contained herein, you are taking full responsibility for your actions. This Book contains information and general advice that is intended to help the readers to be better informed about physical, mental, emotional, and Spiritual wellbeing. Always consult your doctor for your individual needs. This Book is not intended to be a substitute for the medical advice of a licensed physician. The reader should consult with their doctor in any matters relating to his/her health. This Book contains information and general advice about business pursuits. This book is not intended to be a substitute for financial or legal advice. Reader is advised to consult your licensed financial or legal professional for such matters. In no event does the author or the publisher make guarantees, express or implied, as to results or consequences arising out of or related to the reader's use or inability to use the book's contents.

Both the author and Highland Light Publishers (the publisher) do not assume and hereby disclaim any liability to any party for any loss, direct, indirect, or consequential damages, accidental, unintentional, or unforeseen, pain, suffering, emotional distress, or disruption resulting from the reader's negligence, actions or non-actions, accident, or any other cause.

The Light of the Soul Foundation is a Charitable
non-profit 501 (c) (3) Philanthropic Organization
founded in 1998 by Gordon Corwin, Trustee.
This non-denominational Foundation is dedicated
to
The Spiritual Enlightenment of Humanity.
LOSF continues to be harmoniously bonded with
Highland Light Publishers,
sharing this Spiritual mission that includes
writing, publishing and distributing Masters'
books in addition to delivering live events with
wisdom from The Ascended Masters Above.

"Bringing the Light of Spirit into the _every-day lives_
and _consciousness_ of the masses
in an increasingly troubled earthly world
… is the practical gift We lovingly offer".

As you now may observe, the collective behavior of Humanity
present dark and pervasive behaviors that prevail
without change. Your kind philanthropy,

donations, and bequests provide the financial means enabling Us to continue serving and delivering *Enlightenment from Above*, expanding Our outreach of Light. Your donations are transformed into the highest vibrations from Above to all Ones aspiring to reach and live their full Dharma's potential of heightened awareness, Love, Compassion and Soul evolution ... which awaits Humanity.

Light of the Soul Foundation

Charitable **N**on-profit 501 (c) (3)

Public Events and Spiritual Counseling

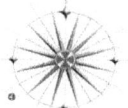

IRS **EIN: 91-1945098**

For Your Gifts, Donations, or Bequest Confirmations, By Debit Card, Credit Card, Check, or Wire

We are deeply grateful to Donors, Contributors and Philanthropists for your fine and generous *Gifts of Grace to uplift The Human Consciousness.*

You are an immensely essential resource that ongoingly empowers Our continuing Outreach.

For two decades, We have delivered gifts of Soul Enlightenment and Practical Spirituality via recently published channeled works, along with

public events and Spiritual readings …
with your generous support.

Many Thanks and Blessings. *You All* are Most Appreciated!
Gratefully yours, Gordon Corwin / Lah Rahn

Contact: Trustee, Gordon Corwin, Oceanside, CA 92056

Gordon@gordoncorwin.com   or
Lah@SaintGermainChrnoicles.com

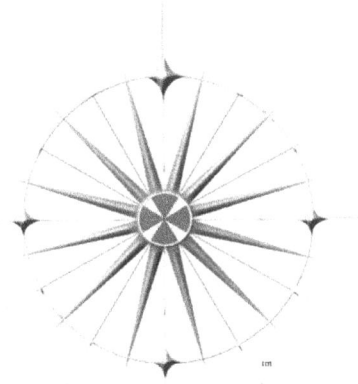

𝔏ight of the 𝔖oul 𝔉oundation

www.SaintGermainChronicles.com

IRS **EIN: 91-1945098**

ACKNOWLEDGEMENTS

To All of those who have so generously contributed their loving, timely, and ongoing support to the success of this book, using your unique creative talents and abilities, artistry, technical skills, financial resources, and much more, please know that YOU are most highly appreciated! Without your support, this book would not have been born into life for all of those who would surround themselves with the dynamics of successful relationships. My heartful thanks goes out to you all, with best wishes for your continued advancement along your Spiritual journey and in your varied careers of endeavor. I send, along with Ascended Master Saint Germain, highest Blessings, admiration and love.

Lah Rahn Ananda
aka Gordon Corwin II

LLantar Chris Gulve, my longtime loyal friend and Spiritual Chela, for your inspiration and support to begin this second book channeling project, dedicated to enlightening Human lives in those many vitally important facets of relationship dynamics that you hold near and dear to your heart. Your selfless and steady encouragement throughout the creation of this book, along with contributing most capable and diligent proof reading of the manuscript, has been of value beyond description. You are acknowledged with the greatest of appreciation, with many grateful thanks from both myself as the Author and Ascended Master Saint Germain and the Realm. Love and Blessings to you.

Jossue Legaspi Aguiere, my brother in this lifetime and Soul compadre over several past lives, I salute you for your enthusiastic willingness to support the creation of this work. Your consciousness and Soul have rapidly grown to be an extraordinary messenger of life's lessons dynamically delivered to the Author in real time during the channeling process of this book. You continue to gift quality experiences of value in friendship, camaraderie and adventure, many of which were and are so very inspirational in creating this work for Humanity. You have my friendship, love and gratitude always.

Tim Yargeau, with special thanks for your kind and enthusiastic co-operation in applying your creative and very effective graphic design and photography skills, just when they were most needed! The results of your fine work, begun with the Saint Germain Chronicles Collection book project, greatly enhancing the true beauty of many graphic displays throughout the book as well. Your many image creations were also used in Saint Germain's new book '*You Me and We, Relationships that Sing to Your Soul*' which has been written and is now in the Publishing process and to be released on Amazon.
t.-yargeau@gmail.com

Teri Rider, for the spectacular graphic design and image creation of the Highland Light Monogram and LOGO, banner and all! And many thanks for the support in successfully publishing RISING ABOVE A Journey Into Higher Dimensions, another of Saint Germain's gems of wisdom now available to Humanity world wide.
www.topreadspublishing.com

Elaine Johnson, my old friend from Junior High School in Highland, California. After many years, we have reconnected and are able to enjoy the past and now present times together. Many thanks for your willing and gracious support in the important proof reading process of publishing this new book! Many Blessings to you.

Marius Michael-George, for the most beautiful licensed, color images of your paintings, presenting likenesses of Ascended Masters Saint Germain and El Morya. Artwork © Marius Michael-George
www.Mariusfineart.com

Dreamstime.com, for your print licensed permission to utilize graphic images that add so much to illustrate text, solely inside the book in various places, with imagination and beauty.
Dreamstime.com

FCIT Florida Center for Instructional Technology, for the licensed use of your copyrighted, beautiful floral, ornate, and decorative capital letters inside of the book.
licensing@fcit.us

123RF Limited, for your beautiful graphic images, print licensed for   Our use, adding so much illustrative vitality in various places, solely inside of the book.
123RF.com

Public Domain, for location of the Comte Saint Germain portrait, and the circa 1864 Charles Sindelar public domain original portrait image of Saint Germain. The Public Domain Review

☙❧

ABOUT THE AUTHOR

ordon Corwin II, also known by his Spiritual vibration as Lah Rahn Ananda, translated literally as 'God Light Messenger', is a native Californian, educated at UC Berkeley, followed by service as a Commissioned US Naval Officer, and by extensive careers in the computer and real estate industries.

In 1995, Gordon clearly heard Lord Saint Germain's mysterious voice Above, to immediately Ascended Spirit Soul's calling to considerable  resounding and and call from recruiting him engage with and follow his reactivate his past life Atlantean DNA channeling abilities, and to begin walking his Dharma to serve Humanity! First as an appointed Masters' Representative and now a Masters' Partner, Lah Rahn delivers Ascended energies through channeling of the Masters' words and visual media, which would now become his changed and conscious life path. In 1998 he founded The Light of the Soul Foundation, a qualified non-profit entity for advanced Spiritual education and Human philanthropy.

Following years of ego-cleansing by the Masters, Lah Rahn Ji has, for over 24 years now, delivered clear and engaging channelings of live public and private Spiritual events, along with potent and enlightening mentoring of Chelas in The Light of the Soul Vortex in Southern California.

In 2007 he was highly honored to be chosen by Lord Saint Germain to be the Ascended Masters' instrument and Partner to begin, and later complete, this precise and accurate channeling to Earth of:

𝕿𝖍𝖊 𝕾𝖆𝖎𝖓𝖙 𝕲𝖊𝖗𝖒𝖆𝖎𝖓 𝕮𝖍𝖗𝖔𝖓𝖎𝖈𝖑𝖊𝖘 𝕮𝖔𝖑𝖑𝖊𝖈𝖙𝖎𝖔𝖓 *2017*.

In ongoing partnership with Lord Saint Germain, Lah Rahn / Gordon Corwin II's second book: *"VICTORY FOR THE SOUL, Relationships That Work",* is being released to the World in 2022 on Amazon as an inspiration to Humanity that relationships can flourish in harmony and Love when merged with the Wisdom of Spirit presented in this new book.

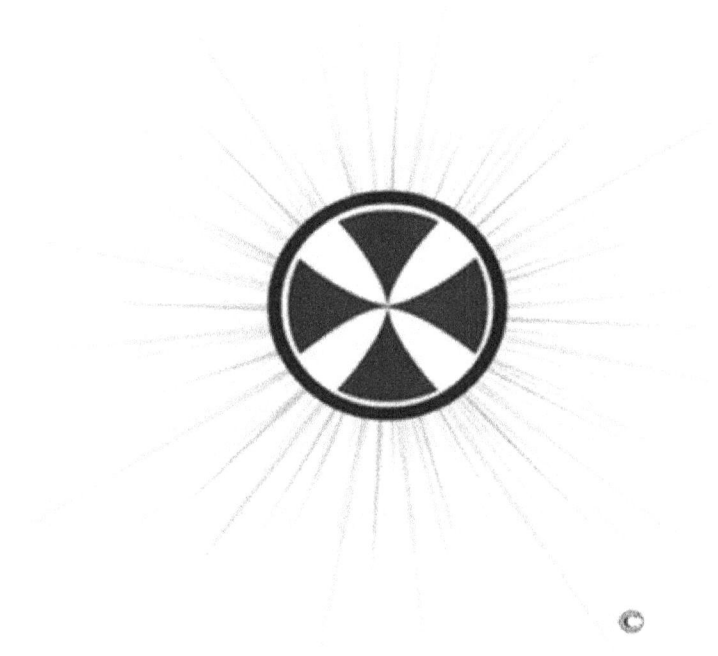

INDEX

A

abilities 47, 69, 102, 120, 265, 289, 339, 343
absolute 55, 149, 193, 229, 270, 295, 320, 329
abstinence 205
abundance 4, 70, 152, 177, 292
acceptance 35, 134, 157, 159, 186, 219, 231, 232, 298
acknowledged 107, 118, 128, 207
acknowledging 159, 212
acknowledgment 186, 278, 298
addictions 204, 207
Admitting 103
Adulthood 217-219
advice 58, 192, 237, 238, 333
agreeing 183, 185, 306
agreement 17, 21, 134, 174, 186, 202
allowed 34, 35, 86, 286
Ambassadors 180
anger 2, 5, 76, 120, 123, 127-130, 132, 133, 137, 208, 233, 248, 249
anger-filled 130, 314
angry 94, 129, 324
angst 223, 228
Archangels 278
arrogance 181
Ascend 128, 199
Ascended 2, 31, 47, 80, 126, 136, 155, 156, 178-180, 220, 222, 227, 241, 250, 277, 278, 280, 282, 305, 307, 312, 335, 339, 341, 343, 344
Ascension 15, 40, 80, 147, 290

Ascensions 126
attachments 42, 64, 150, 195-204, 207, 208, 210, 212, 226, 228, 232, 235, 251, 252, 274
A-u-m 262
aura 46
author 2, 104, 167, 237, 277, 303, 304, 333, 340, 343
automatic 112, 133, 179, 288
automatically 228
automaticity 112, 122
awake 64, 70
awakened 267
axiomatic 4, 185, 199
Ayurvedic 145

B

balance 5, 8, 15, 41, 56, 145, 156, 174, 193, 202, 211, 213, 214, 219, 254
balanced 5, 90, 111, 122, 169, 193, 197, 250
balancing 14, 28, 29, 35, 174, 182
bandage 115, 198
begin 4, 15, 31, 111, 112, 115, 155, 157, 195, 207, 208, 265, 284, 288, 298, 339, 343, 344
behavioral 69, 74, 163
Beingness 197
beliefs 20, 124, 196, 197, 201, 209, 210, 217-219, 224
beware 57, 229, 246, 287
biggie 103
bind 45, 197, 198, 207
binding 162, 200, 203, 211, 213
birthright 13, 125
blend 26, 45, 55, 157, 190, 193
blended 1, 42
blending 56, 63, 78, 194, 223, 310

blessing 40, 47, 73, 88, 156, 157, 238, 265, 272, 284, 294, 304
BLINDED 129
bliss 120, 180, 260
Blissful 273
blocked 94, 129
blueprint 72
bonded 102, 250, 251, 312, 335
Bootcamp 303
breakdown 3, 164, 165, 250
breakthrough 95
breakthroughs 8
breath 131, 238, 253
broken 92, 106, 149, 166, 229, 250, 257
Brotherhood 284
brothers 47, 256
build 244
building 4, 31, 39, 45, 104, 139, 168, 173, 244, 251, 304, 325
bumps 133, 242
burdensome 125, 154
button 102, 104, 105
buttons 101-103, 109, 113
bytes 47

C

calloused 256
candidate 175, 176
capability 33, 36, 188, 189
career 90, 111
carelessness 167
celebrate 117, 183, 275, 282, 321
celebration 285

chakra 28, 29, 192
chakras 28, 179, 288
challenge 5, 26, 103, 121, 145, 150, 195, 245, 257
changed 94, 245, 292, 344
changes 95, 148, 235, 257, 299
channel 270, 277, 304, 305
channelings 344
Channelship 277
childhood 104
children 244, 283
choosers 156, 291
chosen 125, 129, 219, 238, 290, 291, 300, 305, 344
clearing 165, 185, 189, 232
clinging 95, 144, 176, 210
clutch 251, 312
collective 64, 79, 80, 187, 190, 218, 219, 282, 289, 298, 299, 335
commitment 12, 36, 181, 229, 230, 311
communicate 73, 94, 105, 169, 185, 325
communicating 183, 326
compassion 2, 52, 59, 62, 155, 157-160, 165, 189, 223, 232, 235, 270, 286, 336
compassionate 159
competing 288, 298
competition 79, 279, 280, 282-288, 291-297, 299
competitive 77, 296
competitors 292
completion 95, 222, 247, 251
completions 59, 90, 224, 238, 255, 271
concordance 97
concurrently 222, 231
confession 103
confidence 29, 182
conflicting 76, 84
confrontational 107, 273

connect 56, 65, 173, 201
conscious 25, 47, 64, 70, 90, 96, 112, 121, 124, 126, 135, 152, 158, 176, 201, 223, 228, 229, 237, 248, 253, 254, 258, 260, 265, 269, 305, 344
consciously 12, 26, 33, 42, 52, 91, 126, 141, 180, 182, 191, 204, 258, 259, 271, 287
consciousnesses 56, 194, 310
consideration 21, 22, 63, 112, 121, 127, 131, 167, 169, 173, 183, 306
constant 150, 178, 292
constructive 121, 130, 132, 133, 205, 207
convoluted 219, 223, 292
correction 88, 139, 206, 282
courage 44, 45, 58, 118, 192, 202, 235
courageous 103, 201, 286
cravings 205
creating 55, 100, 131, 132, 159, 171, 176, 193, 238, 269, 340
creation 76, 140, 172, 314, 339, 340
creations 340
creative 181, 188, 306, 339, 340
creator 155, 268, 289, 291, 299, 333
Creator's 277
crown 278, 288
cultural 218, 304
cultures 158, 304
custom 283
customs 287, 299
cycles 95, 257

D

daily 4, 5, 25, 32, 47, 48, 62, 122, 123, 136, 145, 232, 260, 265, 294, 305

dangerous 135
darkness 29, 226
dating 255
daunting 63, 282
deceive 100
deceived 94, 108
decisions 4, 70, 182
Decree 139, 261
Decrees 60, 61, 260
defuse 307
delusion 197
demanding 71, 108, 109
demands 64, 136, 163, 165, 166, 183, 218, 231, 292
demonstrate 128, 219
demonstration 278, 296
desperate 176, 196
detached 32, 222, 231, 273
Detaching 237, 238, 242
detachment 134, 151, 165, 186, 197, 200, 201, 209-211, 214, 223, 224, 226, 227, 231, 235, 238, 241-246, 248, 250, 251, 253, 254, 258, 260, 270, 273, 300, 322
Detachments 210, 305
dharma 29, 199
Dharma's 336
difference 49, 71, 76, 131, 234
dignify 270, 320
dilemmas 32, 79
diligence 13, 37, 307
discern 112, 328
discipline 2, 5, 57, 64, 76, 93, 110, 124, 126, 128, 149, 229, 250
discovery 201, 271
dividends 145
divinely 71, 84, 134, 152, 156, 186, 191, 290, 327

dominant 213
dominate 127, 200
dominated 196, 200, 205, 217
dominating 205, 233, 280, 292
drama 31, 92, 129, 159, 207, 208, 229, 304
drink 219, 247, 313
Duality 77, 79, 80, 176, 177, 252, 294, 299

E

ego-based 299
Ego-bound 213
egocentrism 181
ego-cleansing 344
Ego-dominant 213
Ego-dominated 212
Ego-filled 129
Egos 26, 97, 127, 162, 219, 223-225, 227, 229, 284, 296, 318, 319
Ego-sourced 199
elder 244
elders 218
elemental 147
elevating 209
embody 211, 267
embraced 71, 220, 289, 291
embracing 5, 45, 280, 283, 284
emotion 126-128, 132, 135, 137-139, 149, 150, 168, 233, 246, 260
empowerment 159
emptiness 137, 245
empty 275
emulate 80
encapsulate 45, 212

encourage 5, 64, 152, 164, 182
engage 14, 29, 41, 42, 122, 226, 285, 343
engulfed 217
enjoying 133
enjoyment 48
enlighten 102, 277
enlightened 13, 133, 141, 180, 190, 278, 285, 304, 311
enlightening 207, 280, 339, 344
enlightenment 5, 47, 86, 129, 136, 224, 283, 304, 335, 336
enraptured 8
enthusiasm 4, 15, 32, 123, 209, 249, 284, 299-301
envy 285, 289
eons 198, 284, 292
escalate 73
escalated 71, 132
escalating 65, 137, 167, 187
essential 2, 32, 36, 61, 162, 173, 299, 336
essentials 36, 45, 202, 304
esteem 63, 296
eternal 276, 315
ethereal 47
ethers 58, 60, 79, 192, 280
ethical 112
ethics 112
euphoria 123
euphoric 8
everlasting 196
everyone 176, 286, 294
everything 106, 184
evolution 26, 45, 112, 115, 147, 148, 156, 201, 210, 242, 300
evolved 102, 146, 197, 284, 287, 292, 295, 311, 324
evolving 2, 285, 299
excuse 127, 162

excuses 106, 149, 204, 229, 286
exercise 62
exhausted 227
exonerated 200
expand 33, 174, 211, 212, 229, 277, 287
expanded 195, 201
expanding 272
expectation 93, 104
expectations 93, 108, 231, 232, 253
experiences 20, 33, 104, 120, 130, 195, 225, 232, 247, 287, 313, 340

F

faces 4, 16, 169, 176, 177, 180, 183, 222
facets 26, 180, 339
failed 284, 295
fair 62, 108
faith 12, 134, 152, 166, 186, 234, 294
faithful 103
family 14, 20, 104, 217-219
fear 72, 78, 79, 111, 120, 121, 214
fears 178, 196, 201
feed 96
feeding 204, 242
feeling 21, 40, 42, 58, 72, 105, 124, 144, 180, 192, 221, 245, 275, 285
Finalogue 280
financial 333, 339
flesh 250, 312
flexible 147, 183
Flight 132
flood 28, 47, 109, 122, 125, 126
flourish 4, 12, 70, 185, 344

focused 37, 89, 167, 269, 280, 287, 292, 293
focusing 174, 177, 178, 183
foolhardy 296
foolish 156
forceful 78, 200
forcefully 33, 213, 228
forever-binding 251, 312
forgive 131, 132, 243
forgiven 243
forgiveness 2, 5, 45, 69, 94, 155-160, 223, 232, 270
foundation 42, 162, 244, 335-337, 344
freedom 8, 13, 34, 47, 52, 86, 87, 95, 129, 151, 152, 154, 160, 196, 197, 201, 207, 209, 213, 219, 226-228, 243, 246, 251, 257, 261, 274, 275, 285, 287, 300, 310, 329
Freedoms 227, 252, 254
Freedom's 34
free-will 42, 86, 110, 120, 156, 157, 180, 193, 200, 208-210, 212, 222, 242, 266, 290, 291, 294, 299, 300, 330
friendships 11, 26
frustration 123, 127, 132, 137
frustrations 254
fulfill 72, 238
fulfilled 71, 80
fulfillment 1, 177, 203
full-hearted 12, 134, 186, 311
fundamental 2, 36, 39, 45, 71, 199, 201, 218, 291, 304
fundamentals 3, 4, 139, 166, 172, 202, 270, 300

G

Gabriel 278
gate 21

gates 177
gateway 12, 120, 122, 136, 300
gateways 37
generational 163, 164, 218
generous 108, 336
Germain's 70, 277, 278, 280, 303, 309, 340, 343
Ghosted 107
Ghosters 256
ghosting 165, 255
gift 1, 13, 34, 40, 47, 88, 128, 156, 160, 180, 222, 238, 266, 271, 283, 335, 340
gifts 2-4, 45, 50, 76, 102, 118, 141, 229, 249, 269, 336
glass 59, 139
global 283, 284
Globe 145, 279, 283, 284, 304
glorified 287, 294, 296
God-given 121
God's 152, 261, 263, 264, 278
golden 36, 81, 146, 187, 283, 300
gordoncorwin 337
Graceful 251
gracefully 12, 33, 222
gracious 40, 341
grandness 13
grasp 93, 104, 147, 251, 312
grateful 34, 120, 238, 259, 277, 278, 306, 336
gratefulness 226
gratitude 2, 128, 152, 224, 249, 275-277, 315, 327, 340
greed 111, 121, 175
grisly 97
grizzly 318
ground 15, 97, 145, 228
grounded 97, 99, 145
groundwork 244

grow 1, 48, 176, 183, 209, 211
grudge 208
Guidebooks 37, 278
guided 137, 177, 191
guideline 218
guidelines 148, 174
guides 266, 289
guiding 12, 37, 45, 47, 88, 287, 333

H

haaaa 139, 195
habit 70, 133, 148, 157, 205, 245, 247, 250
habits 91, 100, 202, 203, 245, 258, 286
habitual 87, 92, 126, 132, 229, 245, 258
habitually 96, 244
Half-assed 234, 327
half-empty 139
half-full 139
halfway 286
Half-wits 161
handle 120, 128, 189, 257
handled 185, 190
handling 52, 126, 133
happiness 1, 14, 64, 87, 99, 102, 201, 214, 216, 249, 271, 307, 323, 327
harmonious 102, 120, 181, 255
harmoniously 289, 335
harmonize 122, 157
harmonizing 280
harmony 3, 51, 63, 102, 111, 123, 134, 166, 168, 172, 173, 176, 186, 188, 199, 216, 219, 244, 295, 344
HARVEST 154
hate 76, 120, 123

haunting 92
heal 102, 113, 324
healed 149, 198, 273
healing 5, 8, 35, 61, 62, 103, 105, 112, 113, 126, 129, 133, 137, 149, 223, 238, 246, 260, 265, 269, 270
healings 4, 102
heals 61
health 29, 90, 152, 248, 333
health-responsible 61
healthy 15, 86, 102, 145, 165, 172, 174, 182, 202, 203, 297, 322
heartache 4
heartful 151, 158, 162, 181, 234, 235, 249, 251, 278, 339
heart-space 295
heart-touching 260
heartwarming 70
hemorrhaging 227
higher-self 32, 43-45, 60, 146, 157, 187, 203, 274, 289, 307
Highest-Self 65, 140
Hilarion 278
Holy 112, 140, 262, 263, 265
honest 17, 48, 96, 97, 103, 105, 224, 286, 304, 306, 322
honestly 50, 224, 230
honesty 42, 64, 112, 146, 162, 229
honor 60, 111, 140, 169, 297, 298, 305
honorable 289
honored 62, 344
honoring 52
honors 86
hope 14, 115, 238
hopefully 34, 223, 224, 228, 305
host 69, 156, 196, 258

hot-button 102
Human-kind 284
humble 63
humbling 103
humorous 5

I

ideal 52, 224
illuminate 198
illusion 15, 16, 32, 44, 45, 87, 91, 97, 134, 159, 185, 197, 198, 200, 213, 228, 233, 248, 250, 252, 253, 258, 293, 297, 299, 310, 318, 320
illusions 19, 120, 122, 201, 252
impatience 132, 137
impatient 233, 257
importance 32, 34, 58, 69, 112, 120, 249, 296, 297
incarceration 229
incluso 161
Inconsiderate 109
inconvenient 16
incorrigible 219
incubate 71, 315
indulge 227
indulgence 126, 127, 129, 130, 197, 200, 227, 248, 314
indulging 129, 198, 205
infinite 277
inflammatory 228
ingrained 112, 176, 230
ingredients 45, 97, 162, 184, 223, 318
inspiration 13, 15, 59, 62, 123, 192, 209, 286, 303, 339, 344
inspirational 340
inspirations 266

inspire 211
inspired 304
inspiring 26
instrument 2, 3, 31, 47, 280, 344
integrate 5, 47, 88, 222
integrity 21, 36, 106, 199, 231
interlocking 3
intermesh 111, 168
interwoven 277
intimacy 40
intimate 283
intuition 17, 306
intuitive 202
involved 4, 80, 187, 193, 223, 233, 244, 246, 291
iron 5
ironic 51
issue 59, 113, 130, 159, 165, 185, 229, 251

J

jealousy 285, 289
Jesus 46, 47, 278, 290
Jossue 340
journeying 219
journeys 4, 172
joyful 8, 141, 220, 286
joyfully 12, 59, 140, 154, 177, 192, 249, 267
joys 22, 224, 261, 269, 275, 297, 307, 315
judge 287, 297
judged 105, 233, 293, 294, 296, 297
judgment 34, 79, 130, 133, 210, 285, 291, 295, 296, 298, 300, 329
judgmental 89, 217
juicy 200

justifiable 106, 109, 213

K

Karma 3, 5, 14, 15, 35, 50, 115, 120, 223, 225, 300
Karmic 14, 15, 126, 127, 155, 198, 199, 212, 213, 225, 256
Keen 328
keys 132, 299
kindness 105, 162, 298
knee-jerk 187

L

ladder 32, 80, 127, 128, 179, 296
landscape 12
layers 50, 64
liberated 37
liberation 44, 310
Liberations 1
license 202
life-lesson 256
life-stream 2, 35, 41, 58, 71, 149, 188, 192, 212, 219, 238, 284, 299
life-streams 121, 283
lifestyle 70
light-hearted 21
loved 39, 90, 128, 152, 195, 232, 233, 237
lovers 4, 14, 32
loves 26, 195, 200
Love's 180
loving 12, 55, 63, 71, 125, 147, 152, 156, 160, 193, 285, 339
lovingly 3, 52, 220, 237, 242, 335

lower 89, 129, 152, 156, 179, 242, 258, 296
loyalty 193, 197, 230
lubricate 259
lurk 32
lurking 149
lyric 176

M

maelstrom 164
magic 15, 179, 180, 214
magical 59, 71, 177, 180, 192, 253
magically 1, 157, 212, 321
managed 122, 125, 128, 260
mandatory 162, 185, 314
manifest 72, 248
manifestation 71, 148, 188, 189
manifestations 333
manifested 123
manifesting 29, 156
manifests 63, 90
manipulate 127
manipulated 94
man-made 79, 252
mantra 37, 188, 265
marriage 4
marvelous 17, 270
masses 127, 145, 177, 335
Masterful 13, 47
Mastering 1, 2, 86, 102, 151, 157, 195, 231, 238
Masters 47, 58, 70, 80, 278, 307, 335, 341, 344
Mastery 1, 4, 8, 40, 102, 103, 121-123, 129, 136, 141,
    170, 179, 202, 205, 210, 212-214, 300, 319
meditate 145, 232

meditating 96, 145
meditation 57, 61, 90, 136, 145, 176, 265
Meditative 136
Meditator 137
memorization 139
mental 92, 333
mentor 243
Mercy 262
mindboggling 71
miracle 319
miracles 59
moment 15, 25, 32-34, 74, 81, 88, 100, 115, 124, 126, 129, 134, 140, 152, 154, 162, 174, 176, 186, 187, 197, 201, 211, 223, 228, 230, 237, 261, 263, 267, 270, 280, 307, 314
momentarily 122
momentary 126, 200
moments 5, 8, 22, 33, 34, 37, 48, 90, 102, 129, 139, 149, 187, 197, 211, 226, 231, 244, 261, 263, 266, 267, 285, 315
money 79, 196, 205, 232, 233
monstrous 79
morphed 79, 284
motivated 121, 234
motivation 11, 18, 128
moves 127, 134, 186, 187, 248
moving 48, 151, 159, 165, 176, 199, 223, 224, 226, 228, 230, 232, 238, 246, 250, 269, 271, 273, 274
Moving-On 165, 275
multidimensional 198
mysterious 70, 71, 115, 280, 343
mystery 51, 71

N

Nada 278
Narcissism 41, 174, 175, 181, 212, 318
Narcissist 213
narcissistic 63, 106, 108, 176, 181
Narcissist's 212
nectar 247, 313
neutral 91, 110, 260
neutralize 260
nirvana 13
non-evolution 218
non-evolvement 218
Non-Judgment 210
NonJudgments 322
notes 111
nourished 173, 183
nourishment 234
nurturing 26, 62

O

objectives 210, 224
Obligation 60
obligations 52
oblivious 127, 196, 213, 228
observation 34, 126, 130, 133, 198
obsessed 196, 251, 292, 312
obsession 41, 61, 91, 92, 97, 205, 229
obsessive-compulsive 258
octave 86, 322
octaves 277, 293
offensive 112
Oneness 1, 15, 40, 56, 79, 126, 191, 212, 214, 241,
    278-280, 282-290, 294, 295, 299-301

opening 14, 65, 120, 198, 212, 257, 259, 271, 282
openings 25, 33, 199
openness 2, 4, 37, 151, 177
opinion 33, 34, 130, 159, 185
opinions 20, 120, 158, 183, 189, 196, 201, 320
opportunities 1, 15, 63, 72, 123, 176, 187, 275, 300
opposites 70, 193, 252
optimistic 12, 15, 97, 99
optimum 188
ordinary 45
outcome 71, 72, 89, 93, 150, 176, 197, 211, 218, 223, 231, 232, 285, 287, 291, 295-297
overall 62, 179, 180, 188, 218, 284, 298, 300
over-enthusiasm 20
overindulgence 61
overlapping 42, 64, 193
overpowering 4
overrunning 205
overshined 48
owned 102
ownership 12, 13, 306

P

painful 93, 125, 180, 200
Paradigm 279, 280, 282, 283, 285, 287, 288, 300
paramount 55, 91, 193, 304
parent 219
participant 280, 291
participants 181, 283, 285, 293
participate 288, 290, 298
participation 285-287, 289, 294, 295, 297, 298, 301
partnership 2, 15, 31, 32, 34-37, 40, 43, 44, 72, 112, 140, 172, 184, 189, 190, 242, 244, 310, 344

partnerships 4, 31
partner's 7, 174, 175
passion 11, 209, 211, 217, 219, 221
passive-aggressive 165, 166, 189
patient 57, 73, 133
patiently 74, 280
perception 16, 267, 280, 299, 312
permission 61, 127, 341
perpetuity 247
perseverance 29, 70, 73
philosophy 176, 289, 294
physical 4, 210, 333
physically 248
pleasantries 90
pleasurable 125, 172
plodder 149
polish 111
polished 195
polishing 303
Ponder 79, 197, 219
pop-off 127
portal 14, 185, 300, 327
portals 192
possession 64
possessiveness 214
possibilities 2, 150, 258, 259, 275, 333
possibility 159, 187, 232, 293
practical 1, 169, 235, 278, 283, 289, 335, 336
practices 155, 160, 182
prayer 71, 226, 266
prison 41, 175, 318
prisoner 97, 208, 318
procrastination 166
productive 172
productivity 102

profound 12, 238
progress 22, 23, 64, 111, 117, 122, 199, 201, 205, 207, 208, 210, 252
promises 21, 62, 106, 166, 200, 223
purged 185
Purification 299
purpose 36, 63, 103, 111, 154, 169, 185, 221, 269, 271
purposeful 166
purposes 162, 166, 333
puzzle 2, 3, 270, 280

Q

qualities 69, 73, 232
quintessential 46, 88
quitting 221, 233
Quotation 122
QUOTATIONS 309

R

rankings 296
ransom 41, 318
react 49, 109, 111, 131
reaction 95, 113, 119, 130, 132, 133, 166
reactions 22, 25, 89, 112, 121, 122, 130, 135, 314
reactivate 343
reactivated 249
reactivation 158, 245, 248, 250, 270, 271
reactive 89, 103, 135, 187
realistic 32, 97, 176
realities 11, 16, 19, 224, 230, 258, 287
reciprocating 277
reciprocity 14, 180, 327

recommitting 166
reconcile 156
re-discovering 48
refinement 283
refinements 283
Refuse 226
refused 105
refuses 165
regression 260
regret 208
relationship's 274
re-scrambled 250
resolutions 90, 224, 229
responsibility 52, 86, 125, 159, 168, 333
responsible 21, 128, 152, 199, 211, 219, 285
rest 157, 227, 260, 265, 300, 305
restfully 146, 273
revelations 45, 50
risk 257
risks 219
romance 11
routine 62, 147, 230, 232
routines 145, 232
rung 32, 80, 179
rungs 127, 128, 179
rush 74
rushed 163
rushing 73, 167, 315
ruthless 283, 284

S

sacred 41, 60, 112, 155, 175, 252, 264, 271, 297
sacrifice 122

sadly 218, 255, 284
sadness 208
sage 58, 192
SaintGermainChrnoicles 337
SaintGermainChronicles 46, 281, 337
SaintGermanChronicles 301, 330
satisfaction 32, 76, 105, 123, 127, 200, 252, 263, 285, 288, 294
satisfied 134, 186, 229, 293, 295
self-absorbed 212
self-acknowledge 88
self-actualization 333
self-awareness 139, 201
self-care 64
self-centered 102, 127
Self-commitment 146
self-deception 50, 197, 320
self-defeating 89
self-discipline 100
self-discovery 48, 49, 333
self-drama 92
self-esteem 102, 188
self-examination 2
self-examined 25, 26, 333
self-indulgences 41, 175, 318
self-inspiring 60
selfishness 41, 63, 108, 175, 181
self-love 4, 23, 39-42, 44, 45, 48, 52, 55, 58, 59, 61, 63, 64, 69, 88, 139, 165, 175-177, 202, 209, 225, 238, 248, 256, 269, 305, 321
self-loving 41, 55, 61, 193
self-nurturing 43, 60, 61
self-observant 149, 209
self-sabotage 232
self-serving 213

self-talk 5, 43, 45, 60, 83, 86-91, 94-97, 100, 102, 104,
    139, 148, 149, 158, 247, 321, 322
sensitive 101, 193, 209
sexual 202, 205, 232
shackled 41, 175, 217, 318
shackles 275
shifting 95, 96, 145, 210, 280, 322
shine 29, 44, 112, 131, 152, 170, 177
Soul 1-3, 5, 14, 25, 35, 69, 117, 120, 150, 162, 172,
    188, 196, 211, 219, 223, 242, 256, 257, 266, 278,
    280, 289, 295, 304, 309, 327, 335-337, 340, 344
Soul-self 150, 222, 225
sourced 134, 185, 186, 188, 237, 279, 285, 307
space 1, 3, 21, 33, 46, 48, 59, 63, 76, 115, 124, 137,
    146, 157, 171, 172, 177, 181, 183, 190, 198, 210,
    214, 232, 241, 242, 253, 254, 257, 271, 275, 289,
    307, 311, 314, 324
spectrum 3
speed 133, 189, 223, 242
speedbumps 73
Spirit-seekers 280, 283, 298
strengthen 13, 316
strengths 181
stubborn 41, 96, 175, 213, 219, 318
stubbornness 166
successes 299, 301
success-filled 36
successful 31, 89, 102, 231, 339
suffering 93, 95, 197, 201, 209, 221, 230, 232, 233,
    238, 245, 248, 249, 253, 334
sufficient 62, 272
suggested 187
suggestions 295, 307
sullenness 166
superior 287, 292

supportive 62, 238
surrender 96, 134, 139, 150, 186, 231, 260, 285, 300, 319, 328
surrendered 47, 196, 275
survival 78, 79, 284, 292, 293
survive 145, 292
synchronicities 55, 118, 249, 285
synchronicity 50, 71, 148, 172, 285
synchronizing 168

T

teachings 35, 70, 122, 124, 222
teamwork 52, 102, 190, 311
temperance 61
timeless 277, 278
timeliness 57
timely 73, 248, 339
togetherness 3, 102, 183, 285
tolerance 177
toolbox 157, 329
transcend 80, 154, 177, 219, 246, 287, 294, 296, 299
transcended 78, 136, 278, 280, 289
transcendental 61, 136
transcending 47, 122, 139, 199, 270, 294
transformation 333
transformed 123
trigger 50, 103, 109, 111, 114, 138, 208
triggered 102, 110, 113, 138, 249
triggering 101, 115, 149, 247
triggers 4, 49, 101-105, 111-113, 159, 172, 248, 324
trustable 190, 311
trustworthy 267
Truthful 203

truths 16, 104, 193, 289, 304, 333
Tuning 43, 45, 65

U

ubiquitous 147, 304
quite 16
ultimate 2, 46, 55, 156, 193, 211
unawareness 189
unblemished 34
unbreakable 199
uncompromised 231
unconsciously 33
undelivered 93, 94, 104, 165
understandable 3, 92, 238, 245
understood 71, 169
Ungrateful 107
unhappy 213
union 1, 172, 173, 175, 223
unique 55, 160, 188, 251, 278, 287, 339
unison 79, 177
unity 1, 172, 190, 278, 285
Universal 3, 219, 251, 275, 277, 300
universe 3, 15, 25, 42, 46, 55, 64, 71, 72, 115, 147, 152, 155, 156, 163, 188, 191, 195, 203, 209, 214, 229, 274, 277, 291, 294-296
Universes 147, 264
unmanaged 125
un-Mastered 14
UNWIND 61
uplifted 86, 298
upset 22, 58, 59, 93-98, 104, 132, 133, 148, 189, 192, 252, 253, 314, 318
upsets 45, 92, 93, 104, 138, 148, 165, 254

V

vibrate 21
vibrating 76
vibrational 2, 46, 89, 103, 117, 120, 149, 151, 152, 257, 258, 277, 293
vibrations 21, 43, 45, 62, 65, 112, 121, 139, 155, 156, 167, 224, 245, 258, 280, 285, 336
victories 13, 117, 183
victory 1-3, 69, 263, 278, 280, 289, 291, 304, 309, 344
viewpoint 188, 297
vigor 11, 126, 209, 300
virtuous 69
visceral 88, 125, 227
viscerally 69, 289
vulnerable 224, 257

W

wake-up 62
wants 18, 21, 43, 45, 51-54, 61, 62, 71, 72, 76, 134, 183, 186, 196, 199, 202-205, 207, 293, 305
willful 166
willingly 12, 29, 45, 122, 201, 231, 306, 329
Wisdom-laced 280
wonders 252, 277
wondrous 8, 46, 52, 253, 277
Worldwide 283
worth 49, 91, 96, 117, 154
worthiness 127

Y

yang 190
young 145, 217-219

Z

Zadkiel 278
zone 91, 110, 119, 128, 146, 149, 205, 260, 289, 311, 324
zones 91, 110, 139